Google Cloud Platform

Associate Cloud Engineer

Practice Exam Questions 2021

Anthony Stewart

Associate Cloud Engineer Practice Test

Question #1

What is the fundamental unit of computing in cloud computing?

1. Physical server
2. VM
3. Block
4. Subnet

Correct Answer(s):

VM

Question #2

If you use a cluster that is managed by a cloud provider, which of these will be managed for you by the cloud provider?

1. Monitoring
2. Networking
3. Some security management tasks
4. All of the above

Correct Answer(s):

All of the above

Question #3

You need serverless computing for file processing and running the backend of a website; which two products can you choose from Google Cloud Platform?

1. Kubernetes Engine and Compute Engine

2. App Engine and Cloud Functions
3. Cache
4. Network File System

Correct Answer(s):

App Engine and Cloud Functions

Question #4

You have been asked to design a storage system for a web application that allows users to upload large data files to be analyzed by a business intelligence workflow. The files should be stored in a high-availability storage system. File system functionality is not requireWhich storage system in Google Cloud Platform should be used?

1. Block storage
2. Object storage
3. Cache
4. Network File System

Correct Answer(s):

Object storage

Question #5

All block storage systems use what block size?

1. 4KB
2. 8KB
3. 16KB
4. Block size can vary.

Correct Answer(s):

Block size can vary.

Question #6

You have been asked to set up network security in a virtual private clouYour company wants to have multiple subnetworks and limit traffic between the subnetworks. Which network security control would you use to control the flow of traffic between subnets?

1. Identity access management
2. Router
3. Firewall
4. IP address table

Correct Answer(s):

Correct Answer(s):

Firewall

Question #7

When you create a machine learning service to identify text in an image, what type of servers should you use to manage compute resources?

1. VMs
2. Clusters of VMs
3. No servers; specialized services are serverless
4. VMs running Linux only

Correct Answer(s):

No servers; specialized services are serverless

Question #8

Investing in servers for extended periods of time, such as committing to use servers for three to five years, works well when?

1. A company is just starting up

3

2. A company can accurately predict server need for an extended period of time
3. A company has a fixed IT budget
4. A company has a variable IT budget

Correct Answer(s):

A company can accurately predict server need for an extended period of time

Question #9

Your company is based in X and will be running a virtual server for Y. What factor determines the unit per minute cost?

1. The time of day the VM is run
2. The characteristics of the server
3. The application you run
4. None of the above

Correct Answer(s):

The characteristics of the server

Question #10

You plan to use Cloud Vision to analyze images and extract text seen in the image. You plan to process between 1,000 and 2,500 images per hour. How many VMs should you allocate to meet peak demand?

1. 1
2. 10
3. 25
4. None; Cloud Vision is a serverless service.

Correct Answer(s):

None; Cloud Vision is a serverless service.

Question #11

You have to run a number of services to support an application. Which of the following is a good deployment model?

1. Run on a large, single VM
2. Use containers in a managed cluster
3. Use two large VMs, making one of them read only
4. Use a small VM for all services and increase the size of the VM when CPU utilization exceeds 90 percent

Correct Answer(s):

Use containers in a managed cluster

Question #12

You have created a VM. Which of the following system administration operations are you allowed to perform on it?

1. Configure the file system
2. Patch operating system software
3. Change file and directory permissions
4. All of the above

Correct Answer(s):

All of the above

Question #13

Cloud Filestore is based on what file system technology?

1. Network File System (NFS)
2. XFS
3. EXT4
4. ReiserFS

Correct Answer(s):

Network File System (NFS)

Question #14

When setting up a network in GCP, your network the resources in it are treated as what?

1. Virtual private cloud
2. Subdomain
3. Cluster
4. None of the above

Correct Answer(s):

Virtual private cloud

Question #15

You need to store data for X and therefore you are using a cache for Y. How will the cache affect data retrieval?

1. A cache improves the execution of client-side JavaScript.
2. A cache will continue to store data even if power is lost, improving availability.
3. Caches can get out of sync with the system of truth.
4. Using a cache will reduce latency, since retrieving from a cache is faster than retrieving from SSDs or HDDs.

Correct Answer(s):

Using a cache will reduce latency, since retrieving from a cache is faster than retrieving from SSDs or HDDs.

Question #16

Why can cloud providers offer elastic resource allocation?

1. Cloud providers can take resources from lower-priority customers and give them to higher-priority customers.
2. Extensive resources and the ability to quickly shift resources between customers enables public cloud providers to offer elastic resource allocation more efficiently than can be done in smaller data centers.
3. They charge more the more resources you use.
4. They don't.

Correct Answer(s):

Extensive resources and the ability to quickly shift resources between customers enables public cloud providers to offer elastic resource allocation more efficiently than can be done in smaller data centers.

Question #17

What is not a characteristic of specialized services in Google Cloud Platform?

1. They are serverless; you do not need to configure servers or clusters.
2. They provide a specific function, such as translating text or analyzing images.
3. They require monitoring by the user.
4. They provide an API to access the functionality of the service.

Correct Answer(s):

They require monitoring by the user.

Question #18

Your client's transactions must access a drive attached to a VM that allows for random access to parts of files. What kind of storage does the attached drive provide?

1. Object storage
2. Block storage
3. NoSQL storage
4. Only SSD storage

Correct Answer(s):

Block storage

Question #19

You are deploying a new relational database to support a web application. Which type of storage system would you use to store data files of the database?

1. Object storage
2. Data storage
3. Block storage
4. Cache

Correct Answer(s):

Block storage

Question #20

A user prefers services that require minimal setup; why would you recommend Cloud Storage, App Engine, and Cloud Functions?

1. They are charged only by time.
2. They are serverless.
3. They require a user to configure VMs.
4. They can only run applications written in Go.

Correct Answer(s):

They are serverless.

Question #21

You are planning to deploy a SaaS application for customers in North America, Europe, and AsiTo maintain scalability, you will need to distribute workload across servers in multiple regions. Which GCP service would you use to implement the workload distribution?

1. Cloud DNS
2. Cloud Spanner
3. Cloud Load Balancing
4. Cloud CDN

Correct Answer(s):

Cloud Load Balancing

Question #22

You have decided to deploy a set of microservices using containers. You could install and manage Docker on Compute Engine instances, but you'd rather have GCP provide some container management services. Which two GCP services allow you to run containers in a managed service?

1. App Engine standard environment and App Engine flexible environment
2. Kubernetes Engine and App Engine standard environment
3. Kubernetes Engine and App Engine flexible environment
4. App Engine standard environment and Cloud Functions

Correct Answer(s):

Kubernetes Engine and App Engine flexible environment

Question #23

Why would an API developer want to use the Apigee API platform?

1. To get the benefits of routing and rate-limiting
2. Authentication services

3. Version control of code
4. A and B
5. E. All of the above

Correct Answer(s):

A and B

Question #24

You are deploying an API to the public Internet and are concerned that your service will be subject to DDoS attacks. Which GCP service should you consider to protect your API?

1. Cloud Armor
2. Cloud CDN
3. Cloud IAM
4. VPCs

Correct Answer(s):

Cloud Armor

Question #25

You have an application that uses a Pub/Sub message queue to maintain a list of tasks that are to be processed by another application. The application that consumes messages from the Pub/Sub queue removes the message only after completing the task. It takes approximately 10 seconds to complete a task. It is not a problem if two or more VMs perform the same task. What is a cost-effective configuration for processing this workload?

1. Use preemptible VMs
2. Use standard VMs
3. Use DataProc
4. Use Spanner

Correct Answer(s):

Use preemptible VMs

Question #26

Your department is deploying an application that has a database backenYou are concerned about the read load on the database server and want to have data available in memory to reduce the time to respond to queries and to reduce the load on the database server. Which GCP service would you use to keep data in memory?

1. Cloud SQL
2. Cloud Memorystore
3. Cloud Spanner
4. Cloud Datastore

Correct Answer(s):

Cloud Memorystore

Question #27

The Cloud SDK can be used to configure and manage resources in which of the following services?

1. Compute Engine
2. Cloud Storage
3. Network firewalls
4. All of the above

Correct Answer(s):

All of the above

Question #28

What server configuration is required to use Cloud Functions?

1. VM configuration
2. Cluster configuration
3. Pub/Sub configuration
4. None

Correct Answer(s):

None

Question #29

You have been assigned the task of consolidating log data generated by each instance of an

application. Which of the Stackdriver management tools would you use?

1. Monitoring
2. Trace
3. Debugger
4. Logging

Correct Answer(s):

Logging

Question #30

Which specialized services are most likely to be used to build a data warehousing platform that requires complex extraction, transformation, and loading operations on batch data as well as processing streaming data?

1. Apigee API platform
2. Data analytics
3. AI and machine learning
4. Cloud SDK

Correct Answer(s):

Data analytics

Question #31

Your company has deployed 100,000 Internet of Things (IoT) sensors to collect data on the state of equipment in several factories. Each sensor will collect and send data to a data store every 5 seconds. Sensors will run continuously. Daily reports will produce data on the maximum, minimum, and average value for each metric collected on each sensor. There is no need to support transactions in this application. Which database product would you recommend?

1. Cloud Spanner
2. Cloud Bigtable
3. Cloud SQL MySQL
4. Cloud SQL PostgreSQL

Correct Answer(s):

Cloud Bigtable

Question #32

You are the lead developer on a medical application that uses patients' smartphones to capture biometric datThe app is required to collect data and store it on the smartphone when data cannot be reliably transmitted to the backend application. You want to minimize the amount of development you have to do to keep data synchronized between smartphones and backend data stores. Which data store option should you recommend?

1. Cloud Firestore
2. Cloud Spanner
3. Cloud Datastore
4. Cloud SQL

Correct Answer(s):

Cloud Firestore

Question #33

A software engineer comes to you for a recommendation. She has implemented a machine learning algorithm to identify cancerous cells in medical images. The algorithm is computationally intensive, makes many mathematical calculations, requires immediate access to large amounts of data, and cannot be easily distributed over multiple servers. What kind of Compute Engine configuration would you recommend?

1. High memory, high CPU
2. High memory, high CPU, GPU
3. Mid-level memory, high CPU
4. High CPU, GPU

Correct Answer(s):

High memory, high CPU, GPU

Question #34

You are tasked with mapping the authentication and authorization policies of your on-premises applications to GCP's authentication and authorization mechanisms. The GCP documentation states that an identity must be authenticated in order to grant privileges to that identity. What does the term identity refer to?

1. VM ID
2. User
3. Role
4. Set of privileges

Correct Answer(s):

User

Question #35

A client is developing an application that will need to analyze large volumes of text information. The client is not expert in text mining or working with language. What GCP service would you recommend they use?

1. Cloud Vision
2. Cloud ML
3. Cloud Natural Language Processing
4. Cloud Text Miner

Correct Answer(s):

Cloud Natural Language Processing

Question #36

Data scientists in your company want to use a machine learning library available only in Apache Spark. They want to minimize the amount of administration and DevOps work. How would you recommend they proceed?

1. Use Cloud Spark
2. Use Cloud Dataproc
3. Use BigQuery
4. Install Apache Spark on a cluster of VMs

Correct Answer(s):

Use Cloud Dataproc

Question #37

Database designers at your company are debating the best way to move a database to GCP. The database supports an application with a global user base. Users expect support for transactions and the ability to query data using commonly used query tools. The database designers decide that any database service they choose will need to support ANSI 2011 and global transactions. Which database service would you recommend?

1. Cloud SQL
2. Cloud Spanner
3. Cloud Datastore
4. Cloud Bigtable

Correct Answer(s):

Cloud Spanner

Question #38

Which specialized service supports both batch and stream processing workflows?

1. Cloud Dataproc
2. BigQuery
3. Cloud Datastore
4. AutoML

Correct Answer(s):

Cloud Dataproc

Question #39

You have a Python application you'd like to run in a scalable environment with the least amount of management overheaWhich GCP product would you select?

1. App Engine flexible environment
2. Cloud Engine
3. App Engine standard environment
4. Kubernetes Engine

Correct Answer(s):

App Engine standard environment

Question #40

A product manager at your company reports that customers are complaining about the reliability of one of your applications. The application is crashing periodically, but developers have not found a common pattern that triggers the crashes. They are concerned that they do not have good insight into the behavior of the application and want to perform a detailed review of all crash datWhich Stackdriver tool would you use to view consolidated crash information?

1. Dataproc
2. Monitoring
3. Logging
4. Error Reporting

Correct Answer(s):

Error Reporting

Question #41

You are designing cloud applications for a healthcare provider. The records management application will manage medical information for patients. Access to this data is limited to a small number of employees. The billing department application will have insurance and payment information. Another group of employees will have access billing information. In addition, the billing system will have two components: a private insurance billing system and a government payer billing system. Government regulations require that software used to bill the government must be isolated from other software systems. Which of the following resource hierarchies would meet these requirements and provide the most flexibility to adapt to changing requirements?

1. One organization, with folders for records management and billing. The billing folder would have private insurer and government payer folders within it. Common constraints would be specified in organization-level policies. Other policies would be defined at the appropriate folder.
2. One folder for records management, one for billing, and no organization. Policies defined at the folder level.
3. One organization, with folders for records management, private insurer, and government payer below the organization. All constraints would be specified in organization-level policies. All folders would have the same policy constraints.

17

4. None of the above.

Correct Answer(s):

One organization, with folders for records management and billing. The billing folder would have private insurer and government payer folders within it. Common constraints would be specified in organization-level policies. Other policies would be defined at the appropriate folder.

Question #42

When you create a hierarchy, you can have more than one of which structure?

1. Organization only
2. Folder only
3. Folder and project
4. Project only

Correct Answer(s):

Folder and project

Question #43

You are designing an application that uses a series of services to transform data from its original form into a format suitable for use in a data warehouse. Your transformation application will write to the message queue as it processes each input file. You don't want to give users permission to write to the message queue. You could allow the application to write to the message queue by using which of the following?

1. Billing account
2. Service account
3. Messaging account
4. Folder

Question #44

Your company has a number of policies that need to be enforced for all projects. You decide to apply policies to the resource hierarchy. Not long after you apply the policies, an engineer finds that an application that had worked prior to implementing policies is no longer working. The engineer would like you to create an exception for the application. How can you override a policy inherited from another entity in the resource hierarchy?

1. Inherited policies can be overridden by defining a policy at a folder or project level.
2. Inherited policies cannot be overridden.
3. Policies can be overridden by linking them to service accounts.
4. Policies can be overridden by linking them to billing accounts.

Correct Answer(s):

Inherited policies can be overridden by defining a policy at a folder or project level.

Question #45

Constraints are used in resource hierarchy policies. Which of the following are types of constraints allowed?

1. Allow a specific set of values
2. Deny a specific set of values
3. Deny a value and all its child values
4. Allow all allowed values
5. All of the above

Correct Answer(s):

All of the above

Question #46

A team with four members needs you to set up a project that needs only general permissions for all resources. You are granting each person a primitive role for different levels of access, depending on their responsibilities in the project. Which of the following are not included as primitive roles in Google Cloud Platform?

1. Owner
2. Publisher
3. Editor
4. Viewer

Correct Answer(s):

Publisher

Question #47

You are deploying a new custom application and want to delegate some administration tasks to DevOps engineers. They do not need all the privileges of a full application administrator, but they do need a subset of those privileges. What kind of role should you use to grant those privileges?

1. Primitive
2. Predefined
3. Advanced
4. Custom

Correct Answer(s):

Custom

Question #48

An app for a finance company needs access to a database and a Cloud Storage bucket. There is no predefined role that grants all the needed permissions without granting some permissions that are not needeYou decide to create a custom role. When defining custom roles, you should follow which of the following principles?

1. Rotation of duties
2. Least principle
3. Defense in depth
4. Least privilege

Correct Answer(s):

Least privilege

Question #49

How many organizations can you create in a resource hierarchy?

1. 1
2. 2
3. 3
4. Unlimited

Correct Answer(s):

1

Question #50

You are contacted by the finance department of your company for advice on how to automate payments for GCP services. What kind of account would you recommend setting up?

1. Service account
2. Billing account
3. Resource account
4. Credit account

Question #51

Correct Answer(s):

Billing account

You are experimenting with GCP for your company. You do not have permission to incur costs. How can you experiment with GCP without incurring charges?

1. You can't; all services incur charges.
2. You can use a personal credit card to pay for charges.
3. You can use only free services in GCP.
4. You can use only serverless products, which are free to use.

Correct Answer(s):

You can use only free services in GCP.

Question #52

Your DevOps team has decided to use Stackdriver monitoring and logging. You have been asked to set up Stackdriver workspaces. When you set up a Stackdriver workspace, what kind of resource is it associated with?

1. A Compute Engine instance only
2. A Compute Engine instance or Kubernetes Engine cluster only
3. A Compute Engine instance, Kubernetes Engine cluster, or App Engine app
4. A project

Correct Answer(s):

A project

Question #53

A large enterprise is planning to use GCP across a number of subdivisions. Each subdivision is managed independently and has its own budget. Most subdivisions plan to spend tens of thousands of dollars per month. How would you recommend they set up their billing account(s)?

1. Use a single self-service billing account.
2. Use multiple self-service billing accounts.
3. Use a single invoiced billing account.
4. Use multiple invoiced billing accounts.

Correct Answer(s):

Use multiple invoiced billing accounts.

Question #54

An application administrator is responsible for managing all resources in a project. She wants to delegate responsibility for several service accounts to another administrator. If additional service accounts are created, the other administrator should manage those as well. What is the best way to delegate privileges needed to manage the service accounts?

1. Grant iam.serviceAccountUser to the administrator at the project level.
2. Grant iam.serviceAccountUser to the administrator at the service account level.
3. Grant iam.serviceProjectAccountUser to the administrator at the project level.
4. Grant iam.serviceProjectAccountUser to the administrator at the service account level.

Correct Answer(s):

Grant iam.serviceAccountUser to the administrator at the project level.

Question #55

You work for a retailer with a large number of brick and mortar stores. Every night the stores upload daily sales datYou have been tasked with creating a service that verifies the uploads every night. You decide to use a service account. Your manager questions the security of your proposed solution, particularly about authenticating the service account. You explain the authentication mechanism used by service accounts. What authentication mechanism is used?

1. Username and password
2. Two-factor authentication
3. Encrypted keys
4. Biometrics

Correct Answer(s):

Encrypted keys

Question #56

What objects in GCP are sometimes treated as resources and sometimes as identities?

1. Billing accounts
2. Service accounts
3. Projects
4. Roles

Correct Answer(s):

Service accounts

Question #57

You plan to develop a web application using products from the GCP that already include established roles for managing permissions such as read-only access or the ability to delete old versions. Which of the following roles offers these capabilities?

1. Primitive roles
2. Predefined roles
3. Custom roles
4. Application roles

Correct Answer(s):

Predefined roles

Question #58

You are reviewing a new GCP account created for use by the finance department. An auditor has questions about who can create projects by default. You explain who has privileges to create projects by default. Who is included?

1. Only project administrators
2. All users
3. Only users without the role resourcemanager.projects.create
4. Only billing account users

Correct Answer(s):

All users

Question #59

How many projects can be created in an account?

1. 10
2. 25
3. There is no limit.
4. Each account has a limit determined by Google.

Correct Answer(s):

Each account has a limit determined by Google.

Question #60

You are planning how to grant privileges to users of your company's GCP account. You need to document what each user will be able to do. Auditors are most concerned about a role called Organization IAM roles. You explain that users with that role can perform a number of tasks, which include all of the following except which one?

1. Defining the structure of the resource hierarchy
2. Determining what privileges a user should be assigned
3. Defining IAM policies over the resource hierarchy
4. Delegating other management roles to other users

Correct Answer(s):

Determining what privileges a user should be assigned

Question #61

You are deploying a Python web application to GCP. The application uses only custom code and basic Python libraries. You expect to have sporadic use of the application for the foreseeable future and want to minimize both the cost of running the application and the DevOps overhead of managing the application. Which computing service is the best option for running the application?

1. Compute Engine
2. App Engine standard environment
3. App Engine flexible environment
4. Kubernetes Engine

Correct Answer(s):

App Engine standard environment

Question #62

Your manager is concerned about the rate at which the department is spending on cloud services. You suggest that your team use preemptible VMs for all of the following except which one?

1. Database server
2. Batch processing with no fixed time requirement to complete
3. High-performance computing cluster
4. None of the above

Correct Answer(s):

Database server

Question #63

What parameters need to be specified when creating a VM in Compute Engine?

1. Project and zone
2. Username and admin role
3. Billing account
4. Cloud Storage bucket

Correct Answer(s):

Project and zone

Question #64

Your company has licensed a third-party software package that runs on Linux. You will run multiple instances of the software in a Docker container. Which of the following GCP services could you use to deploy this software package?

1. Compute Engine only
2. Kubernetes Engine only
3. Compute Engine, Kubernetes Engine, and the App Engine flexible environment only

4. Compute Engine, Kubernetes Engine, the App Engine flexible environment, or the App Engine standard environment

Correct Answer(s):

Compute Engine, Kubernetes Engine, and the App Engine flexible environment only

Question #65

You can specify packages to install into a Docker container by including commands in which file?

1. Docker.cfg
2. Dockerfile
3. Config.dck
4. install.cfg

Correct Answer(s):

Dockerfile

Question #66

How much memory of a node does Kubernetes require as overhead?

1. 10GB to 20GB
2. 1GB to 2GB
3. 1.5GB
4. A scaled amount starting at 25 percent of memory and decreasing to 2 percent of marginal memory as the total amount of memory increases.

Correct Answer(s):

A scaled amount starting at 25 percent of memory and decreasing to 2 percent of marginal memory as the total amount of memory increases.

Question #67

Your manager is making a presentation to executives in your company advocating that you start using Kubernetes Engine. You suggest that the manager highlight all the features Kubernetes provides to reduce the workload on DevOps engineers. You describe several features, including all of the following except which one?

1. Load balancing across Compute Engine VMs that are deployed in a Kubernetes cluster
2. Security scanning for vulnerabilities
3. Automatic scaling of nodes in the cluster
4. Automatic upgrading of cluster software as needed

Correct Answer(s):

Security scanning for vulnerabilities

Question #68

Your company is about to release a new online service that builds on a new user interface experience driven by a set of services that will run on your servers. There is a separate set of services that manage authentication and authorization. A data store set of services keeps track of account information. All three sets of services must be highly reliable and scale to meet demanWhich of the GCP services is the best option for deploying this?

1. App Engine standard environment
2. Compute Engine
3. Cloud Functions
4. Kubernetes Engine

Correct Answer(s):

Kubernetes Engine

Question #69

A mobile application uploads images for analysis, including identifying objects in the image and extracting text that may be embedded in the image. A third party has created the mobile application, and you have developed the image analysis service. You both agree to use Cloud Storage to store images. You want to keep the two services completely decoupled, but you need a way to invoke the image analysis as soon as an image is uploadeHow should this be done?

1. Change the mobile app to start a VM running the image analysis service and have that VM copy the file from storage into local storage on the VM. Have the image service run on the VM.
2. Write a function in Python that is invoked by Cloud Functions when a new image file is written to the Cloud Storage bucket that receives new images. The function should submit the URL of the uploaded file to the image analysis service. The image analysis service will then load the image from Cloud Storage, perform analysis, and generate results, which can be saved to Cloud Storage.
3. Have a Kubernetes cluster running continuously, with one pod dedicated to listing the contents of the upload bucket and detecting new files in Cloud Storage and another pod dedicated to running the image analysis software.
4. Have a Compute Engine VM running and continuously listing the contents of the upload bucket in Cloud Storage to detect new files. Another VM should be continually running the image analysis software.

Correct Answer(s):

Write a function in Python that is invoked by Cloud Functions when a new image file is written to the Cloud Storage bucket that receives new images. The function should submit the URL of the uploaded file to the image analysis service. The image analysis service will then load the image from Cloud Storage, perform analysis, and generate results, which can be saved to Cloud Storage.

Question #70

Your team is developing a new pipeline to analyze a stream of data from sensors on manufacturing devices. The old pipeline occasionally corrupted data because parallel threads overwrote data written by other threads. You decide to use Cloud Functions as part of the pipeline. As a developer of a Cloud Function, what do you have to do to prevent multiple invocations of the function from interfering with each other?

1. Include a check in the code to ensure another invocation is not running at the same time.
2. Schedule each invocation to run in a separate process.
3. Schedule each invocation to run in a separate thread.
4. Nothing. GCP ensures that function invocations do not interfere with each other.

Correct Answer(s):

Nothing. GCP ensures that function invocations do not interfere with each other.

Question #71

A client of yours processes personal and health information for hospitals. All health information needs to be protected according to government regulations. Your client wants to move their application to Google Cloud but wants to use the encryption library that they have used in the past. You suggest that all VMs running the application have the encryption library installeWhich kind of image would you use for that?

1. Custom image
2. Public image
3. CentOS 6 or 7

Correct Answer(s):

Custom image

What is the lowest level of the resource hierarchy?

1. Folder
2. Project
3. File
4. VM instance

Correct Answer(s):

Project

Question #72

Your company is seeing a marked increase in the rate of customer growth in Europe. Latency is becoming an issue because your application is running in us-central1. You suggest deploying your services to a region in Europe. You have several choices. You should consider all of the following factors except which one?

1. Cost
2. Latency
3. Regulations
4. Reliability

Correct Answer(s):

Reliability

Question #73

What role gives users full control over Compute Engine instances?

1. Compute Manager role
2. Compute Admin role
3. Compute Manager role
4. Compute Security Admin

Correct Answer(s):

Compute Admin role

Question #74

Which of the following are limitations of a preemptible VM?

1. Will be terminated within 24 hours.
2. May not always be available. Availability may vary across zones and regions.
3. Cannot migrate to a regular VM.
4. All of the above

Correct Answer(s):

All of the above

Question #75

Custom VMs can have up to how many vCPUs?

1. 16
2. 32
3. 64
4. 128

Correct Answer(s):

64

Question #76

When using the App Engine standard environment, which of the following language's runtime is not supported?

1. Java
2. Python
3. C
4. Go

Correct Answer(s):

C

Question #77

Kubernetes reserves CPU resources in percentage of cores available. The percentage is what range?

1. 1 percent to 10 percent
2. 0.25 percent to 6 percent
3. 0.25 percent to 2 percent
4. 10 percent to 12 percent

0.25 percent to 6 percent

Question #78

Kubernetes deployments can be in what states?

1. Progressing, stalled, completed
2. Progressing, completed, failed
3. Progressing, stalled, failed, completed
4. Progressing, stalled, running, failed, completed

Correct Answer(s):

Progressing, completed, failed

Question #79

A client has brought you in to help reduce their DevOps overheaEngineers are spending too much time patching servers and optimizing server utilization. They want to move to serverless platforms as much as possible. Your client has heard of Cloud Functions and wants to use them as much as possible. You recommend all of the following types of applications except which one?

1. Long-running data warehouse data load procedures
2. IoT backend processing
3. Mobile application event processing
4. Asynchronous workflows

Correct Answer(s):

Long-running data warehouse data load procedures

Question #80

You have just opened the GCP console at console.google.com. You have authenticated with the user you want to use. What is one of the first things you should do before performing tasks on VMs?

1. Open Cloud Shell.
2. Verify you can SSH into a VM.
3. Verify that the selected project is the one you want to work with.
4. Review the list of running VMs.

Correct Answer(s):

Verify that the selected project is the one you want to work with.

Question #81

What is a one-time task you will need to complete before using the console?

1. Set up billing
2. Create a project
3. Create a storage bucket
4. Specify a default zone

Correct Answer(s):

Set up billing

Question #82

A colleague has asked for your assistance setting up a test environment in Google ClouThey have never worked in GCP. You suggest starting with a single VM. Which of the following is the minimal set of information you will need?

1. A name for the VM and a machine type
2. A name for the VM, a machine type, a region, and a zone
3. A name for the VM, a machine type, a region, a zone, and a CIDR block
4. A name for the VM, a machine type, a region, a zone, and an IP address

Correct Answer(s):

A name for the VM, a machine type, a region, and a zone

Question #83

An architect has suggested a particular machine type for your workloaYou are in the console creating a VM and you don't see the machine type in the list of available machine types. What could be the reason for this?

1. You have selected the incorrect subnet.
2. That machine type is not available in the zone you specified.
3. You have chosen an incompatible operating system.
4. You have not specified a correct memory configuration.

Correct Answer(s):

That machine type is not available in the zone you specified.

Question #84

Your manager asks for your help with understanding cloud computing costs. Your team runs dozens of VMs for three different applications. Two of the applications are for use by the marketing department and one is use by the finance department. Your manager wants a way to bill each department for the cost of the VMs used for their applications. What would you suggest to help solve this problem?

1. Access controls
2. Persistent disks
3. Labels and descriptions
4. Descriptions only

Correct Answer(s):

Labels and descriptions

Question #85

If you wanted to set the preemptible property using Cloud Console, in which section of the Create An Instance page would you find the option?

1. Availability Policy
2. Identity And API Access
3. Sole Tenancy
4. Networking

Correct Answer(s):

Availability Policy

Question #86

You need to set up a server with a high level of security. You want to be prepared in case of attacks on your server by someone trying to inject a rootkit (a kind of malware that can alter the operating system). Which option should you select when creating a VM?

1. Firewall
2. Shield VM
3. Project-wide SSH keys
4. Boot disk integrity check

Correct Answer(s):

Shield VM

Question #87

All of the following parameters can be set when adding an additional disk through Google Cloud Console, except one. Which one?

1. Disk type
2. Encryption key management
3. Block size
4. Source image for the disk

Correct Answer(s):

Block size

Question #88

You lead a team of cloud engineers who maintain cloud resources for several departments in your company. You've noticed a problem with configuration drift. Some machine configurations are no longer in the same state as they were when createYou can't find notes or documentation on how the changes were made or why. What practice would you implement to solve this problem?

1. Have all cloud engineers use only command-line interface in Cloud Shell.
2. Write scripts using gcloud commands to change configuration and store those scripts in a version control system.
3. Take notes when making changes to configuration and store them in Google Drive.
4. Limit privileges so only you can make changes so you will always know when and why configurations were changed.

Correct Answer(s):

Write scripts using gcloud commands to change configuration and store those scripts in a version control system.

Question #89

When using the Cloud SDK command-line interface, which of the following is part of commands for administering resources in Compute Engine?

1. gcloud compute instances
2. gcloud instances
3. gcloud instances compute
4. None of the above

Correct Answer(s):

gcloud compute instances

Question #90

A newly hired cloud engineer is trying to understand what VMs are running in a particular project. How could the engineer get summary information on each VM running in a project?

1. Execute the command gcloud compute list
2. Execute the command gcloud compute instances list
3. Execute the command gcloud instances list
4. Execute the command gcloud list instances

Correct Answer(s):

Execute the command gcloud compute instances list

Question #91

When creating a VM using the command line, how should you specify labels for the VM?

1. Use the --labels option with labels in the format of KEYS:VALUES.
2. Use the --labels option with labels in the format of KEYS=VALUE.
3. Use the --labels option with labels in the format of KEYS,VALUES.
4. This is not possible in the command line.

Correct Answer(s):

Use the --labels option with labels in the format of KEYS=VALUE.

Question #92

In the boot disk advanced configuration, which operations can you specify when creating a new VM?

1. Add a new disk, reformat an existing disk, attach an existing disk
2. Add a new disk and reformat an existing disk
3. Add a new disk and attach an existing disk
4. Reformat an existing disk and attach an existing disk

Correct Answer(s):

Add a new disk and attach an existing disk

Question #93

You have acquired a 10 GB data set from a third-party research firm. A group of data scientists would like to access this data from their statistics programs written in R. R works well with Linux and Windows file systems, and the data scientists are familiar with file operations in R. The data scientists would each like to have their own dedicated VM with the data available in the VM's file system. What is a way to make this data readily available on a VM and minimize the steps the data scientists will have to take?

1. Store the data in Cloud Storage.
2. Create VMs using a source image created from a disk with the data on it.
3. Store the data in Google Drive.
4. Load the data into BigQuery.

Correct Answer(s):

Create VMs using a source image created from a disk with the data on it.

Question #94

The Network tab of the create VM form is where you would perform which of the following operations?

1. Set the IP address of the VM
2. Add a network interface to the VM
3. Specify a default router
4. Change firewall configuration rules

Correct Answer(s):

Add a network interface to the VM

Question #95

You want to create a VM using the gcloud commanWhat parameter would you include to specify the type of boot disk?

1. boot-disk-type
2. boot-disk
3. disk-type
4. type-boot-disk

Correct Answer(s):

boot-disk-type

Question #96

Which of the following commands will create a VM with four CPUs that is named web-server-1?

1. gcloud compute instances create --machine-type=n1-standard-4 web-server-1
2. gcloud compute instances create --cpus=4 web-server-1
3. gcloud compute instances create --machine-type=n1-standard-4 -instance-name web-server-1

4. gcloud compute instances create --machine-type=n1-4-cpu web-server-1

Correct Answer(s):

gcloud compute instances create --machine-type=n1-standard-4 web-server-1

Question #97

Which of the following commands will stop a VM named web-server-1?

1. gcloud compute instances halt web-server-1
2. gcloud compute instances --terminate web-server1
3. gcloud compute instances stop web-server-1
4. gcloud compute stop web-server-1

Correct Answer(s):

gcloud compute instances stop web-server-1

Question #98

You have just created an Ubuntu VM and want to log into the VM to install some software packages. Which network service would you use to access the VM?

1. FTP
2. SSH
3. RDP
4. ipconfig

Correct Answer(s):

SSH

Question #99

Your management team is considering three different cloud providers. You have been asked to summarize billing and cost information to help the management team compare cost structures between clouds. Which of the following would you mention about the cost of VMs in GCP?

1. VMs are billed in 1-second increments, cost varies with the number of CPUs and amount of memory in a machine type, you can create custom machine types, preemptible VMs cost up to 80 percent less than standard VMs, and Google offers discounts for sustained usage.
2. VMs are billed in 1-second increments and VMs can run up to 24 hours before they will be be shut down.
3. Google offers discounts for sustained usage in only some regions, cost varies with the number of CPUs and amount of memory in a machine type, you can create custom machine types, preemptible VMs cost up to 80 percent less than standard VMs.
4. VMs are charged for a minimum of 1 hour of use and cost varies with the number of CPUs and amount of memory in a machine type.

Correct Answer(s):

VMs are billed in 1-second increments, cost varies with the number of CPUs and amount of memory in a machine type, you can create custom machine types, preemptible VMs cost up to 80 percent less than standard VMs, and Google offers discounts for sustained usage.

Question #100

Which page in Google Cloud Console would you use to create a single instance of a VM?

1. Compute Engine
2. App Engine
3. Kubernetes Engine
4. Cloud Functions

Correct Answer(s):

Compute Engine

Question #101

You view a list of Linux VM instances in the console. All have public IP addresses assigneYou notice that the SSH option is disabled for one of the instances. Why might that be the case?

1. The instance is preemptible and therefore does not support SSH.
2. The instance is stopped.
3. The instance was configured with the No SSH option.
4. The SSH option is never disabled.

Correct Answer(s):

The instance is stopped.

Question #102

You have noticed unusually slow response time when issuing commands to a Linux server, and you decide to reboot the machine. Which command would you use in the console to reboot?

1. Reboot
2. Reset
3. Restart
4. Shutdown followed by Startup

Correct Answer(s):

Reset

Question #103

In the console, you can filter the list of VM instances by which of the following?

1. Labels only
2. Member of managed instance group only
3. Labels, status, or members of managed instance group
4. Labels and status only

Correct Answer(s):

Labels, status, or members of managed instance group

Question #104

You will be building a number of machine learning models on an instance and attaching GPU to the instance. When you run your machine learning models they take an unusually long time to run. It appears that GPU is not being useWhat could be the cause of this?

1. GPU libraries are not installed.
2. The operating system is based on Ubuntu.
3. You do not have at least eight CPUs in the instance.
4. There isn't enough persistent disk space available.

Correct Answer(s):

GPU libraries are not installed.

Question #105

When you add a GPU to an instance, you must ensure that:

1. The instance is set to terminate during maintenance.
2. The instance is preemptible.
3. The instance does not have nonboot disks attached.
4. The instance is running Ubuntu 14.02 or later.

Correct Answer(s):

The instance is set to terminate during maintenance.

Question #106

You are using snapshots to save copies of a 100GB disk. You make a snapshot and then add 10GB of datYou create a second snapshot. How much storage is used in total for the two snapshots (assume no compression)?

1. 210 GB, with 100GB for the first and 110GB for the second
2. 110 GB, with 100GB for the first and 10GB for the second
3. 110 GB, with 110 for the second (the first snapshot is deleted automatically)
4. 221 GB, with 100GB for the first, 110GB for the second, plus 10 percent of the second snapshot (11 GB) for metadata overhead

Correct Answer(s):

110 GB, with 100GB for the first and 10GB for the second

Question #107

You have decided to delegate the task of making backup snapshots to a member of your team. What role would you need to grant to your team member to create snapshots?

1. Compute Image Admin
2. Storage Admin
3. Compute Snapshot Admin
4. Compute Storage Admin

Correct Answer(s):

Compute Storage Admin

Question #108

The source of an image may be:

1. Only disks
2. Snapshots or disks only

3. Disks, snapshots, or another image
4. Disks, snapshots, or any database export file

Correct Answer(s):

Disks, snapshots, or another image

Question #109

You have built images using Ubuntu 14.04 and now want users to start using Ubuntu 16.04. You don't want to just delete images based on Ubuntu 14.04, but you want users to know they should start using Ubuntu 16.04. What feature of images would you use to accomplish this?

1. Redirection
2. Deprecated
3. Unsupported
4. Migration

Correct Answer(s):

Deprecated

Question #110

You want to generate a list of VMs in your inventory and have the results in JSON format. What command would you use?

1. gcloud compute instances list
2. gcloud compute instances describe
3. gcloud compute instances list --format json
4. gcloud compute instances list --output json

Correct Answer(s):

gcloud compute instances list --format json

Question #111

You would like to understand details of how GCP starts a virtual instance. Which optional parameter would you use when starting an instance to display those details?

1. --verbose
2. --async
3. --describe
4. --details

Correct Answer(s):

--async

Question #112

Which command will delete an instance named ch06-instance-3?

1. gcloud compute instances delete instance=ch06-instance-3
2. gcloud compute instance stop ch06-instance-3
3. gcloud compute instances delete ch06-instance-3
4. gcloud compute delete ch06-instance-3

Correct Answer(s):

gcloud compute instances delete ch06-instance-3

Question #113

You are about to delete an instance named ch06-instance-1 but want to keep its boot disk. You do not want to keep other attached disks. What gcloud command would you use?

1. gcloud compute instances delete ch06-instance-1 --keep-disks=boot
2. gcloud compute instances delete ch06-instance-1 --save-disks=boot
3. gcloud compute instances delete ch06-instance-1 --keep-disks=filesystem
4. gcloud compute delete ch06-instance-1 --keep-disks=filesystem

Correct Answer(s):

gcloud compute instances delete ch06-instance-1 --keep-disks=boot

Question #114

You want to view a list of fields you can use to sort a list of instances. What command would you use to see the field names?

1. gcloud compute instances list
2. gcloud compute instances describe
3. gcloud compute instances list --detailed
4. gcloud compute instances describe --detailed

Correct Answer(s):

gcloud compute instances describe

Question #115

You are deploying an application that will need to scale and be highly available. Which of these Compute Engine components will help achieve scalability and high availability?

1. Preemptible instances
2. Instance groups
3. Cloud Storage
4. GPUs

Correct Answer(s):

Instance groups

Question #116

Before creating an instance group, you need to create what?

1. Instances in the instance group
2. Instance group template
3. Boot disk image
4. Source snapshot

Correct Answer(s):

Instance group template

Question #117

How would you delete an instance group template using the command line?

1. gcloud compute instances instance-template delete
2. gcloud compute instance-templates delete
3. gcloud compute delete instance-template
4. gcloud compute delete instance-templates

Correct Answer(s):

gcloud compute instance-templates delete

Question #118

What can be the basis for scaling up an instance group?

1. CPU utilization and operating system updates
2. Disk usage and CPU utilization only
3. Network latency, load balancing capacity, and CPU utilization
4. Disk usage and operating system updates only

Correct Answer(s):

Network latency, load balancing capacity, and CPU utilization

Question #119

An architect is moving a legacy application to Google Cloud and wants to minimize the changes to the existing architecture while administering the cluster as a single entity. The legacy application runs on a load-balanced cluster that runs nodes with two different configurations. The two configurations are required because of design decisions made several years ago. The load on the application is fairly consistent, so there is rarely a need to scale up or down. What GCP Compute Engine resource would you recommended using?

1. Preemptible instances
2. Unmanaged instance groups
3. Managed instance groups
4. GPUs

Correct Answer(s):

Unmanaged instance groups

Question #120

A new engineer is asking for clarification about when it is best to use Kubernetes and when to use instance groups. You point out that Kubernetes uses instance groups. What purpose do instance groups play in a Kubernetes cluster?

1. They monitor the health of instances.
2. They create pods and deployments.
3. They create sets of VMs that can be managed as a unit.
4. They create alerts and notification channels.

Correct Answer(s):

They create sets of VMs that can be managed as a unit.

Question #121

What kinds of instances are required to have a Kubernetes cluster?

1. A cluster master and nodes to execute workloads.
2. A cluster master, nodes to execute workloads, and Stackdriver nodes to monitor node health.
3. Kubernetes nodes; all instances are the same.
4. Instances with at least four vCPUs.

Correct Answer(s):

A cluster master and nodes to execute workloads.

Question #122

What is a pod in Kubernetes?

1. A set of containers
2. Application code deployed in a Kubernetes cluster
3. A single instance of a running process in a cluster
4. A controller that manages communication between clients and Kubernetes services

Correct Answer(s):

A single instance of a running process in a cluster

Question #123

You have developed an application that calls a service running in a Kubernetes cluster. The service runs in pods that can be terminated if they are unhealthy and replaced with other pods that might have a different IP address. How should you code your application to ensure it functions properly in this situation?

1. Query Kubernetes for a list of IP addresses of pods running the service you use.

2. Communicate with Kubernetes services so applications do not have to be coupled to specific pods.
3. Query Kubernetes for a list of pods running the service you use.
4. Use a gcloud command to get the IP addresses needed.

Correct Answer(s):

Communicate with Kubernetes services so applications do not have to be coupled to specific pods.

Question #124

You have noticed that an application's performance has degraded significantly. You have recently made some configuration changes to resources in your Kubernetes cluster and suspect that those changes have alerted the number of pods running in the cluster. Where would you look for details on the number of pods that should be running?

1. Deployments
2. Stackdriver
3. ReplicaSet
4. Jobs

Correct Answer(s):

ReplicaSet

Question #125

You are deploying a high availability application in Kubernetes Engine. You want to maintain availability even if there is a major network outage in a data center. What feature of Kubernetes Engine would you employ?

1. Multiple instance groups
2. Multizone/region cluster
3. Regional deployments
4. Load balancing

Correct Answer(s):

Multizone/region cluster

Question #126

You want to write a script to deploy a Kubernetes cluster with GPUs. You have deployed clusters before, but you are not sure about all the required parameters. You need to deploy this script as quickly as possible. What is one way to develop this script quickly?

1. Use the GPU template in the Kubernetes Engine cloud console to generate the gcloud command to create the cluster
2. Search the Web for a script
3. Review the documentation on gcloud parameters for adding GPUs
4. Use an existing script and add parameters for attaching GPUs

Correct Answer(s):

Use the GPU template in the Kubernetes Engine cloud console to generate the gcloud command to create the cluster

Question #127

What gcloud command will create a cluster named ch07-cluster-1 with four nodes?

1. gcloud beta container clusters create ch07-cluster-1 --num-nodes=4
2. gcloud container beta clusters create ch07-cluster-1 --num-nodes=4
3. gcloud container clusters create ch07-cluster-1 --num-nodes=4
4. gcloud beta container clusters create ch07-cluster-1 4

Correct Answer(s):

gcloud container clusters create ch07-cluster-1 --num-nodes=4

Question #128

When using Create Deployment from Cloud Console, which of the following cannot be specified for a deployment?

1. Container image
2. Application name
3. Time to live (TTL)
4. Initial command

Correct Answer(s):

Time to live (TTL)

Question #129

Deployment configuration files created in Cloud Console use what type of file format?

1. CSV
2. YAML
3. TSV
4. JSON

Correct Answer(s):

YAML

Question #130

What command is used to run a Docker image on a cluster?

1. gcloud container run
2. gcloud beta container run
3. kubectl run
4. kubectl beta run

Correct Answer(s):

kubectl run

Question #131

What command would you use to have 10 replicas of a deployment named

ch07-app-deploy?

1. kubectl upgrade deployment ch07-app-deploy --replicas=5
2. gcloud containers deployment ch07-app-deploy --replicas=5
3. kubectl scale deployment ch07-app-deploy --replicas=10
4. kubectl scale deployment ch07-app-deploy --pods=5

Correct Answer(s):

kubectl scale deployment ch07-app-deploy --replicas=10

Question #132

Stackdriver is used for what operations on Kubernetes clusters?

1. Notifications only
2. Monitoring and notifications only
3. Logging only
4. Notifications, monitoring, and logging

Correct Answer(s):

Notifications, monitoring, and logging

Question #133

Before monitoring a Kubernetes cluster, what must you create with Stackdriver?

1. Log

2. Workspace
3. Pod
4. ReplicaSet

Correct Answer(s):

Workspace

Question #134

What kind of information is provided in the Details page about an instance in Stackdriver?

1. CPU usage only
2. Network traffic only
3. Disk I/O, CPU usage, and network traffic
4. CPU usage and disk I/O

Correct Answer(s):

Disk I/O, CPU usage, and network traffic

Question #135

When creating an alerting policy, what can be specified?

1. Conditions, notifications, and time to live
2. Conditions, notifications, and documentation
3. Conditions only
4. Conditions, documentation, and time to live

Correct Answer(s):

Conditions, notifications, and documentation

Question #136

Your development team needs to be notified if there is a problem with applications running on several Kubernetes clusters. Different team members prefer different notification methods in addition to Stackdriver alerting. What is the most efficient way to send notifications and meet your team's requests?

1. Set up SMS text messaging, Slack, and email notifications on an alert.
2. Create a separate alert for each notification channel.
3. Create alerts with email notifications and have those notification emails forwarded to other notification systems.
4. Use a single third-party notification mechanism.

Correct Answer(s):

Set up SMS text messaging, Slack, and email notifications on an alert.

Question #137

A new engineer is trying to set up alerts for a Kubernetes cluster. The engineer seems to be creating a large number of alerts and you are concerned this is not the most efficient way and will lead to more maintenance work than requireYou explain that a more efficient way is to create alerts and apply them to what?

1. One instance only
2. An instance or entire group
3. A group only
4. A pod

Correct Answer(s):

An instance or entire group

Question #138

You are attempting to execute commands to initiate a deployment on a Kubernetes cluster.

The commands are not having any effect. You suspect that a Kubernetes component is not functioning correctly. What component could be the problem?

1. The Kubernetes API
2. A StatefulSet
3. Cloud SDK gcloud commands
4. ReplicaSet

Correct Answer(s):

The Kubernetes API

Question #139

You have deployed an application to a Kubernetes cluster. You have noticed that several pods are starved for resources for a period of time and the pods are shut down. When resources are available, new instantiations of those pods are createClients are still able to connect to pods even though the new pods have different IP addresses from the pods that were terminateWhat Kubernetes component makes this possible?

1. Services
2. ReplicaSet
3. Alerts
4. StatefulSet

Correct Answer(s):

Services

Question #140

You are running several microservices in a Kubernetes cluster. You've noticed some performance degradation. After reviewing some logs, you begin to think the cluster may be improperly configured, and you open Cloud Console to investigate. How do you see the details of a specific cluster?

1. Type the cluster name into the search bar.

2. Click the cluster name.
3. Use the gcloud cluster details command.
4. None of the above.

Correct Answer(s):

Click the cluster name.

Question #141

You are viewing the details of a cluster in Cloud Console and want to see how many vCPUs are available in the cluster. Where would you look for that information?

1. Node Pools section of the Cluster Details page
2. Labels section of the Cluster Details page
3. Summary line of the Cluster Listing page
4. A and C

Correct Answer(s):

A and C

Question #142

You have been assigned to help diagnose performance problems with applications running on several Kubernetes clusters. The first thing you want to do is understand, at a high level, the characteristics of the clusters. Which command should you use?

1. gcloud container list
2. gcloud container clusters list
3. gcloud clusters list
4. None of the above

Correct Answer(s):

gcloud container clusters list

Question #143

When you first try to use the kubectl command, you get an error message indicating that the resource cannot be found or you cannot connect to the cluster. What command would you use to try to eliminate the error?

1. gcloud container clusters access
2. gcloud container clusters get-credentials
3. gcloud auth container
4. gcloud auth container clusters

Correct Answer(s):

gcloud container clusters get-credentials

Question #144

An engineer recently joined your team and is not aware of your team's standards for creating clusters and other Kubernetes objects. In particular, the engineer has not properly labeled several clusters. You want to modify the labels on the cluster from Cloud Console. How would you do it?

1. Click the Connect button.
2. Click the Deploy menu option.
3. Click the Edit menu option.
4. Type the new labels in the Labels section.

Correct Answer(s):

Click the Edit menu option.

Question #145

You receive a page in the middle of the night informing you that several services running on a Kubernetes cluster have high latency when responding to API requests. You review monitoring data and determine that there are not enough resources in the cluster to keep up with the loaYou decide to add six more VMs to the cluster. What parameters will you need to specify when you issue the cluster resize command?

1. Cluster size
2. Cluster name
3. Node pool name
4. All of the above

Correct Answer(s):

All of the above

Question #146

You want to modify the number of pods in a cluster. What is the best way to do that?

1. Modify pods directly
2. Modify deployments
3. Modify node pools directly
4. Modify nodes

Correct Answer(s):

Modify deployments

Question #147

You want to see a list of deployments. Which option from the Kubernetes Engine navigation menu would you select?

1. Clusters

2. Storage
3. Workloads
4. Deployments

Correct Answer(s):

Workloads

Question #148

What actions are available from the Actions menu when viewing deployment details?

1. Scale and Autoscale only
2. Autoscale, Expose, and Rolling Update
3. Add, Modify, and Delete
4. None of the above

Correct Answer(s):

Autoscale, Expose, and Rolling Update

Question #149

What is the command to list deployments from the command line?

1. gcloud container clusters list-deployments
2. gcloud container clusters list
3. kubectl get deployments
4. kubectl deployments list

Correct Answer(s):

kubectl get deployments

Question #150

What parameters of a deployment can be set in the Create Deployment page in Cloud Console?

1. Container image
2. Cluster name
3. Application name
4. All of the above

Correct Answer(s):

All of the above

Question #151

Where can you view a list of services when using Cloud Console?

1. In the Deployment Details page
2. In the Container Details page
3. In the Cluster Details page
4. None of the above

Correct Answer(s):

In the Deployment Details page

Question #152

What kubectl command is used to add a service?

1. run
2. start
3. initiate
4. deploy

Correct Answer(s):

run

Question #153

You are supporting machine learning engineers who are testing a series of classifiers. They have five classifiers, called ml-classifier-1, ml-classifier-2, etThey have found that ml- classifier-3 is not functioning as expected and they would like it removed from the cluster. What would you do to delete a service called ml-classifier-3?

1. Run the command kubectl delete service ml-classifier-3.
2. Run the command kubectl delete ml-classifier-3.
3. Run the command gcloud service delete ml-classifier-3.
4. Run the command gcloud container service delete ml-classifier-3.

Correct Answer(s):

Run the command kubectl delete service ml-classifier-3.

Question #154

What service is responsible for managing container images?

1. Kubernetes Engine
2. Compute Engine
3. Container Registry
4. Container Engine

Correct Answer(s):

Container Registry

Question #155

What command is used to list container images in the command line?

1. gcloud container images list
2. gcloud container list images
3. kubectl list container images
4. kubectl container list images

Correct Answer(s):

gcloud container images list

Question #156

A data warehouse designer wants to deploy an extraction, transformation, and load process to Kubernetes. The designer provided you with a list of libraries that should be installed, including drivers for GPUs. You have a number of container images that you think may meet the requirements. How could you get a detailed description of each of those containers?

1. Run the command gcloud container images list details.
2. Run the command gcloud container images describe.
3. Run the command gcloud image describe.
4. Run the command gcloud container describe.

Correct Answer(s):

Run the command gcloud container images describe.

Question #157

You have just created a deployment and want applications outside the cluster to have access

to the services provided by the deployment. What do you need to do to the service?

1. Give it a public IP address.
2. Issue a kubectl expose deployment command.

3. Issue a gcloud expose deployment command.
4. Nothing, making it accessible must be done at the cluster level.

Correct Answer(s):

Issue a kubectl expose deployment command.

Question #158

You have deployed an application to a Kubernetes cluster that processes sensor data from a fleet of delivery vehicles. The volume of incoming data depends on the number of vehicles making deliveries. The number of vehicles making deliveries is dependent on the number

of customer orders. Customer orders are high during daytime hours, holiday seasons, and when major advertising campaigns are run. You want to make sure you have enough nodes running to handle the load, but you want to keep your costs down. How should you configure your Kubernetes cluster?

1. Deploy as many nodes as your budget allows.
2. Enable autoscaling.
3. Monitor CPU, disk, and network utilization and add nodes as necessary.
4. Write a script to run gcloud commands to add and remove nodes when peaks usually start and end, respectively.

Correct Answer(s):

Enable autoscaling.

Question #159

When using Kubernetes Engine, which of the following might a cloud engineer need to configure?

1. Nodes, pods, services, and clusters only
2. Nodes, pods, services, clusters, and container images
3. Nodes, pods, clusters, and container images only
4. Pods, services, clusters, and container images only

Question #160

You have designed a microservice that you want to deploy to production. Before it can be deployed, you have to review how you will manage the service lifecycle. The architect is particularly concerned about how you will deploy updates to the service with minimal disruption. What aspect of App Engine components would you use to minimize disruptions during updates to the service?

1. Services
2. Versions
3. Instance groups
4. Instances

Question #161

You've just released an application running in App Engine StandarYou notice that there are peak demand periods in which you need up to 12 instances, but most of the time 5 instances are sufficient. What is the best way to ensure that you have enough instances to meet demand without spending more than you have to?

1. Configure your app for autoscaling and specify max instances of 12 and min instances of 5.
2. Configure your app for basic scaling and specify max instances of 12 and min instances of 5.
3. Create a cron job to add instances just prior to peak periods and remove instances after the peak period is over.
4. Configure your app for instance detection and do not specify a max or minimum number of instances.

Correct Answer(s):

Configure your app for autoscaling and specify max instances of 12 and min instances of 5.

Question #162

In the hierarchy of App Engine components, what is the lowest-level component?

1. Application
2. Instance
3. Version
4. Service

Correct Answer(s):

Instance

Question #163

What command should you use to deploy an App Engine app from the command line?

1. gcloud components app deploy
2. gcloud app deploy
3. gcloud components instances deploy
4. gcloud app instance deploy

Correct Answer(s):

gcloud app deploy

Question #164

You have deployed a Django 1.5 Python application to App Engine. This version of Django requires Python 3. For some reason, App Engine is trying to run the application using Python 2. What file would you check and possibly modify to ensure that Python 3 is used with this application?

1. app.config
2. app.yaml
3. services.yaml
4. deploy.yaml

Correct Answer(s):

app.yaml

Question #165

You have several App Engine apps you plan to deploy from your project. What have you failed to account for in this design?

1. App Engine only supports one app per project.
2. App Engine only supports two apps per project.
3. App Engine apps exist outside of projects.
4. Nothing, this is a common pattern.

Correct Answer(s):

App Engine only supports one app per project.

Question #166

The latest version of your microservice code has been approved by your manager, but the product owner does not want the new features released until a press release is publisheYou'd like to get the code out but not expose it to customers. What is the best way to get the code out as soon as possible without exposing it to customers?

1. Deploy with gcloud app deploy --no-traffic.
2. Write a cron job to deploy after the press release is published.
3. Deploy with gcloud app deploy --no-promote.
4. Deploy as normal after the press release is published.

Correct Answer(s):

Deploy with gcloud app deploy --no-promote.

Question #167

You have just deployed an app that hosts services that provide the current time in any time zone. The project containing the code is called current-time-zone, the service providing the user interface is called time-zone-ui, and the service performing the calculation is called time-zone-calculate. What is the URL where a user could find your service?

    1.   current-time-zone.appengine.com
    2.   current-time-zone.appspot.com
    3.   time-zone-ui.appspot.com
    4.   time-zone-calculate.appspot.com

Correct Answer(s):

current-time-zone.appspot.com

Question #168

You are concerned that as users make connections to your application, the performance will degrade. You want to make sure that more instances are added to your App Engine application when there are more than 20 concurrent requests. What parameter would you specify in app.yaml?

    1.   max_concurrent_requests
    2.   target_throughput_utilization
    3.   max_instances
    4.   max_pending_latency

Correct Answer(s):

max_concurrent_requests

Question #169

What parameters can be configured with basic scaling?

1. max_instances and min_Rinstances
2. idle_timeout and min_instances
3. idle_timeout and max_instances
4. idle_timeout and target_throughput_utilization

Correct Answer(s):

idle_timeout and max_instances

Question

The runtime parameter in app.yaml is used to specify what?

1. The script to execute
2. The URL to access the application
3. The language runtime environment
4. The maximum time an application can run

Correct Answer(s):

The language runtime environment

Question #170

What are the two kinds of instances available in App Engine Standard?

1. Resident and dynamic
2. Persistent and dynamic
3. Stable and dynamic
4. Resident and nonresident

Correct Answer(s):

Resident and dynamic

Question #171

You work for a startup, and costs are a major concern. You are willing to take a slight performance hit if it will save you money. How should you configure the scaling for your apps running in App Engine?

1. Use dynamic instances by specifying autoscaling or basic scaling.
2. Use resident instances by specifying autoscaling or basic scaling.
3. Use dynamic instances by specifying manual scaling.
4. Use resident instances by specifying manual scaling.

Correct Answer(s):

Use dynamic instances by specifying autoscaling or basic scaling.

Question #172

A team of developers has created an optimized version of a service. This should run 30 percent faster in most cases. They want to roll it out to all users immediately, but you are concerned that the substantial changes need to be released slowly in case there are significant bugs. What can you do to allocate some users to the new version without exposing all users to it?

1. Issue the command gcloud app services set-traffic.
2. Issue the command gcloud instances services set-traffic.
3. Issue the command gcloud app set-traffic.
4. Change the target IP address of the service for some clients.

Correct Answer(s):

Issue the command gcloud app services set-traffic.

Question #173

What parameter to gcloud app services set-traffic is used to specify the method to use when splitting traffic?

1. --split-traffic
2. --split-by
3. --traffic-split
4. --split-method

Correct Answer(s):

--split-by

Question #174

What parameter to gcloud app services set-traffic is used to specify the percentage of traffic that should go to each instance?

1. --split-by
2. --splits
3. --split-percent
4. --percent-split

Correct Answer(s):

--splits

Question #175

You have released a new version of a service. You have been waiting for approval from the product manager to start sending traffic to the new version. You get approval to route traffic to the new version. What parameter to gcloud app services set-traffic is used to specify that traffic should be moved to a newer version of the app?

1. --move-to-new
2. --migrate-to-new

3. --migrate
4. --move

Correct Answer(s):

--migrate

Question #176

The status of what components can be viewed in the App Engine console?

1. Services only
2. Versions only
3. Instances and versions
4. Services, versions, and instances

Correct Answer(s):

Services, versions, and instances

Question #177

What are valid methods for splitting traffic?

1. By IP address only
2. By HTTP cookie only
3. Randomly and by IP address only
4. By IP address, HTTP cookies, and randomly

Correct Answer(s):

By IP address, HTTP cookies, and randomly

Question #178

What is the name of the cookie used by App Engine when cookie-based splitting is used?

1. GOOGID
2. GOOGAPPUID
3. APPUID
4. UIDAPP

Correct Answer(s):

GOOGAPPUID

Question #179

A product manager is proposing a new application that will require several backend services, three business logic services, and access to relational databases. Each service will provide a single function, and it will require several of these services to complete a business task. Service execution time is dependent on the size of input and is expected to take up to 30 minutes in some cases. Which GCP product is a good serverless option for running this related service?

1. Cloud Functions
2. Compute Engine
3. App Engine
4. Cloud Storage

Correct Answer(s):

App Engine

Question #180

You have been asked to deploy a cloud function to reformat image files as soon as they are uploaded to Cloud Storage. You notice after a few hours that about 10 percent of the files are not processed correctly. After reviewing the files that failed, you realize they are all substantially larger than average. What could be the cause of the failures?

1. There is a syntax error in the function code.
2. The wrong runtime was selected.
3. The timeout is too low to allow enough time to process large files.
4. There is a permissions error on the Cloud Storage bucket containing the files.

Correct Answer(s):

The timeout is too low to allow enough time to process large files.

Question #181

When an action occurs in GCP, such as a file being written to Cloud Storage or a message being added to a Cloud Pub/Sub topic, that action is called what?

1. An incident
2. An event
3. A trigger
4. A log entry

Correct Answer(s):

An event

Question #182

All of the following generate events that can be triggered using Cloud Functions, except which one?

1. Cloud Storage
2. Cloud Pub/Sub
3. SSL
4. Firebase

Correct Answer(s):

SSL

Question #183

Which runtimes are supported in Cloud Functions?

1. Node.js 5, Node.js 6, and Node.js 8
2. Node.js 8, Python, and Go
3. Node.js 6, Node.js 8, and Python
4. Node.js 8, Python, and Go

Correct Answer(s):

Node.js 8, Python, and Go

Question #184

An HTTP trigger can be invoked by making a request using which of the following?

1. GET only
2. POST and GET only
3. DELETE, POST, and GET
4. DELETE, POST, REVISE, and GET

Correct Answer(s):

DELETE, POST, and GET

Question #185

What types of events are available to Cloud Functions working with Cloud Storage?

1. Upload or finalize and delete only
2. Upload or finalize, delete, and list only

3. Upload or finalize, delete, and metadata update only
4. Upload or finalize, delete, metadata update, and archive

Correct Answer(s):

Upload or finalize, delete, metadata update, and archive

Question #186

You are tasked with designing a function to execute in Cloud Functions. The function will need more than the default amount of memory and should be applied only when a finalize event occurs after a file is uploaded to Cloud Storage. The function should only apply its logic to files with a standard image file type. Which of the following required features cannot be specified in a parameter and must be implemented in the function code?

1. Cloud function name
2. Memory allocated for the function
3. File type to apply the function to
4. Event type

Correct Answer(s):

File type to apply the function to

Question #187

How much memory can be allocated to a Cloud Function?

1. 128MB to 256MB
2. 128MB to 512MB
3. 128MB to 1GB
4. 128MB to 2GB

Correct Answer(s):

128MB to 2GB

Question #188

How long can a cloud function run by default before timing out?

1. 30 seconds
2. 1 minute
3. 9 minutes
4. 20 minutes

Correct Answer(s):

1 minute

Question #189

You want to create a cloud function to transform audio files into different formats. The audio files will be uploaded into Cloud Storage. You want to start transformations as soon as the files finish uploading. Which trigger would you specify in the cloud function to cause it to execute after the file is uploaded?

1. google.storage.object.finalize
2. google.storage.object.upload
3. google.storage.object.archive
4. google.storage.object.metadataUpdate

Correct Answer(s):

google.storage.object.finalize

Question #190

You are defining a cloud function to write a record to a database when a file in Cloud Storage is archiveWhat parameters will you have to set when creating that function?

1. runtime only
2. trigger-resource only
3. runtime, trigger-resource, trigger-event only

4. runtime, trigger-resource, trigger-event, file-type

Correct Answer(s):

runtime, trigger-resource, trigger-event only

Question #191

You'd like to stop using a cloud function and delete it from your project. Which command would you use from the command line to delete a cloud function?

1. gcloud functions delete
2. gcloud components function delete
3. gcloud components delete
4. gcloud delete functions

Correct Answer(s):

gcloud functions delete

Question #192

You have been asked to deploy a cloud function to work with Cloud Pub/SuAs you review the Python code, you notice a reference to a Python function called base64.b64decode. Why would a decode function be required in a Pub/Sub cloud function?

1. It's not required and should not be there.
2. Messages in Pub/Sub topics are encoded to allow binary data to be used in places where text data is expecteMessages need to be decoded to access the data in the message.
3. It is required to add padding characters to the end of the message to make all messages the same length.
4. The decode function maps data from a dictionary data structure to a list data structure.

Correct Answer(s):

Messages in Pub/Sub topics are encoded to allow binary data to be used in places where text data is expecteMessages need to be decoded to access the data in the message.

Question #193

Which of these commands will deploy a Python cloud function called

pub_sub_function_test?

1. gcloud functions deploy pub_sub_function_test
2. gcloud functions deploy pub_sub_function_test --runtime python37
3. gcloud functions deploy pub_sub_function_test --runtime python37 -- trigger-topic gcp-ace-exam-test-topic
4. gcloud functions deploy pub_sub_function_test --runtime python -- trigger-topic gcp-ace-exam-test-topic

Correct Answer(s):

gcloud functions deploy pub_sub_function_test --runtime python37 --trigger-topic gcp-ace-exam-test-topic

Question #194

When specifying a Cloud Storage cloud function, you have to specify an event type, such as finalize, delete, or archive. When specifying a Cloud Pub/Sub cloud function, you do not have to specify an event type. Why is this the case?

1. Cloud Pub/Sub does not have triggers for event types.
2. Cloud Pub/Sub has triggers on only one event type, when a message is published.
3. Cloud Pub/Sub determines the correct event type by analyzing the function code.
4. The statement in the question is incorrect; you do have to specify an event type with Cloud Pub/Sub functions.

Correct Answer(s):

Cloud Pub/Sub has triggers on only one event type, when a message is published.

Question #195

Your company has a web application that allows job seekers to upload résumé files. Some files are in Microsoft Word, some are PDFs, and others are text files. You would like to store all résumés as PDFs. How could you do this in a way that minimizes the time between upload and conversion and with minimal amounts of coding?

1. Write an App Engine application with multiple services to convert all documents to PDF.
2. Implement a Cloud Function on Cloud Storage to execute on a finalize event. The function checks the file type, and if it is not PDF, the function calls a PDF converter function and writes the PDF version to the bucket that has the original.
3. Add the names of all files to a Cloud Pub/Sub topic and have a batch job run at regular intervals to convert the original files to PDF.
4. Implement a Cloud Function on Cloud Pub/Sub to execute on a finalize event. The function checks the file type, and if it is not PDF, the function calls a PDF converter function and writes the PDF version to the bucket that has the original.

Correct Answer(s):

Implement a Cloud Function on Cloud Storage to execute on a finalize event. The function checks the file type, and if it is not PDF, the function calls a PDF converter function and writes the PDF version to the bucket that has the original.

Question #196

What are options for uploading code to a cloud function?

1. Inline editor
2. Zip upload
3. Cloud source repository
4. All of the above

Correct Answer(s):

All of the above

Question #197

What type of trigger allows developers to use HTTP POST, GET, and PUT calls to invoke a cloud function?

1. HTTP
2. Webhook
3. Cloud HTTP
4. None of the above

Correct Answer(s):

HTTP

Question #198

You are tasked with defining lifecycle configurations on buckets in Cloud Storage. You need to consider all possible options for transitioning from one storage class to another. All of the following transitions are allowed except for one. Which one is that?

1. Nearline to coldline
2. Regional to nearline
3. Multiregional to coldline
4. Regional to multiregional

Correct Answer(s):

Regional to multiregional

Question #199

Your manager has asked for your help in reducing Cloud Storage charges. You know that some of the files stored in Cloud Storage are rarely accesseWhat kind of storage would you recommend for those files?

1. Nearline
2. Regional
3. Coldline
4. Multiregional

Correct Answer(s):

Coldline

Question #200

You are working with a startup developing analytics software for IoT datYou have to be able to ingest large volumes of data consistently and store it for several months. The startup has several applications that will need to query this datVolumes are expected to grow to petabyte volumes. Which database should you use?

1. Cloud Spanner
2. Bigtable
3. BigQuery
4. Datastore

Correct Answer(s):

Bigtable

Question #201

A software developer on your team is asking for your help improving the query performance of a database application. The developer is using a Cloud SQL MySQL, Second Generation instance. Which options would you recommend?

1. Memorystore and SSD persistent disks
2. Memorystore and HDD persistent disks
3. Datastore and SSD persistent disks
4. Datastore and HDD persistent disks

Correct Answer(s):

Memorystore and SSD persistent disks

Question #202

You are creating a set of persistent disks to store data for exploratory data analysis. The disks will be mounted on a virtual machine in the us-west2-a zone. The data is historical data retrieved from Cloud Storage. The data analysts do not need peak performance and are more concerned about cost than performance. The data will be stored in a local relational database. Which type of storage would you recommend?

1. SSDs
2. HDDs
3. Datastore
4. Bigtable

Correct Answer(s):

HDDs

Question #203

Which of the following statements about Cloud Storage is not true?

1. Cloud Storage buckets can have retention periods.
2. Lifecycle configurations can be used to change storage class from regional to multiregional.
3. Cloud Storage does not provide block-level access to data within files stored in buckets.
4. Cloud Storage is designed for high durability.

Correct Answer(s):

Lifecycle configurations can be used to change storage class from regional to multiregional.

Question #204

When using versioning on a bucket, what is the latest version of the object called?

1. Live version
2. Top version
3. Active version
4. Safe version

Correct Answer(s):

Live version

Question #205

A product manager has asked for your advice on which database services might be options for a new application. Transactions and support for tabular data are important. Ideally, the database would support common query tools. What databases would you recommend the product manager consider?

1. BigQuery and Spanner
2. Cloud SQL and Spanner
3. Cloud SQL and Bigtable
4. Bigtable and Spanner

Correct Answer(s):

Cloud SQL and Spanner

Question #206

The Cloud SQL service provides fully managed relational databases. What two types of databases are available in Cloud SQL?

1. SQL Server and MySQL
2. SQL Server and PostgreSQL
3. PostgreSQL and MySQL
4. MySQL and Oracle

Correct Answer(s):

PostgreSQL and MySQL

Question #207

Which of the following Cloud Spanner configurations would have the highest hourly cost?

1. Located in us-central1
2. Located in nam3
3. Located in us-west1-a
4. Located in nam-eur-asia1

Correct Answer(s):

Located in nam-eur-asia1

Question #208

Which of the following are database services that do not require you to specify configuration information for VMs?

1. BigQuery only
2. Datastore only
3. Firebase and Datastore
4. BigQuery, Datastore, and Firebase

Correct Answer(s):

BigQuery, Datastore, and Firebase

Question #209

What kind of data model is used by Datastore?

1. Relational
2. Document
3. Wide-column
4. Graph

Correct Answer(s):

Document

Question #210

You have been tasked with creating a data warehouse for your company. It must support tens of petabytes of data and use SQL for a query language. Which managed database service would you choose?

1. BigQuery
2. Bigtable
3. Cloud SQL
4. SQL Server

Correct Answer(s):

BigQuery

Question #211

A team of mobile developers is developing a new application. It will require synchronizing data between mobile devices and a backend database. Which database service would you recommend?

1. BigQuery
2. Firestore
3. Spanner
4. Bigtable

Correct Answer(s):

Firestore

Question #212

A product manager is considering a new set of features for an application that will require additional storage. What features of storage would you suggest the product manager consider?

1. Read and write patterns only
2. Cost only
3. Consistency and cost only
4. None of the above, they are all relevant considerations.

Correct Answer(s):

None of the above, they are all relevant considerations.

Question #213

What is the maximum size of a Memorystore cache?

1. 100GB
2. 300GB
3. 400GB
4. 50GB

Correct Answer(s):

300GB

Question #214

Once a bucket has its storage class set to coldline, what are other storage classes it can transition to?

1. Regional
2. Nearline
3. Multi-regional
4. None of the above

Correct Answer(s):

None of the above

Question #215

Before you can start storing data in BigQuery, what must you create?

1. A data set
2. A bucket
3. A persistent disk
4. An entity

Correct Answer(s):

A data set

Question #216

What features can you configure when running a Second Generation MySQL database in Cloud SQL?

1. Machine type
2. Maintenance windows
3. Failover replicas
4. All of the above

Question #217

A colleague is wondering why some storage charges are so high. They explain that they have moved all their storage to nearline and coldline storage. They routinely access most of the object on any given day. What is one possible reason the storage costs are higher than expected?

1. Nearline and coldline incur access charges.
2. Transfer charges.
3. Multiregional coldline is more expensive.
4. Regional coldline is more expensive.

Question #218

Cloud SQL is a fully managed relational database service, but database administrators still have to perform some tasks. Which of the following tasks do Cloud SQL users need to perform?

1. Applying security patches
2. Performing regularly scheduled backups
3. Creating databases
4. Tuning the operating system to optimize Cloud SQL performance

Correct Answer(s):

Creating databases

Question #219

Which of the following commands is used to create a backup of a Cloud SQL database?

1. gcloud sql backups create
2. gsutil sql backups create
3. gcloud sql create backups
4. gcloud sql backups export

Correct Answer(s):

gcloud sql backups create

Question #220

Which of the following commands will run an automatic backup at 3:00 a.m. on an instance called ace-exam-mysql?

1. gcloud sql instances patch ace-exam-mysql --backup-start-time 03:00
2. gcloud sql databases patch ace-exam-mysql --backup-start-time 03:00
3. cbt sql instances patch ace-exam-mysql --backup-start-time 03:00
4. bq gcloud sql instances patch ace-exam-mysql --backup-start-time 03:00

Correct Answer(s):

gcloud sql instances patch ace-exam-mysql --backup-start-time 03:00

Question #221

What is the query language used by Datastore?

1. SQL

2. MDX
3. GQL
4. DataFrames

Correct Answer(s):

GQL

Question #222

What is the correct command-line structure to export data from Datastore?

1. gcloud datastore export '[NAMESPACE]' gs://[BUCKET_NAME]
2. gcloud datastore export gs://[BUCKET_NAME]
3. gcloud   datastore   export   --namespaces='[NAMESPACE]'
   gs://[BUCKET_NAME]
4. gcloud   datastore   dump   --namespaces='[NAMESPACE]'
   gs://[BUCKET_NAME]

Correct Answer(s):

gcloud datastore export --namespaces='[NAMESPACE]' gs://[BUCKET_NAME]

Question #223

When you enter a query into the BigQuery query form, BigQuery analyzes the query and displays an estimate of what metric?

1. Time required to enter the query
2. Cost of the query
3. Amount of data scanned
4. Number of bytes passed between servers in the BigQuery cluster

Correct Answer(s):

Amount of data scanned

Question #224

You want to get an estimate of the volume of data scanned by BigQuery from the command

line. Which option shows the command structure you should use?

1. gcloud BigQuery query estimate [SQL_QUERY]
2. bq --location=[LOCATION] query --use_legacy_sql=false --dry_run [SQL_QUERY]
3. gsutil --location=[LOCATION] query --use_legacy_sql=false --dry_run [SQL_QUERY]
4. cbt BigQuery query estimate [SQL_QUERY]

Correct Answer(s):

bq --location=[LOCATION] query --use_legacy_sql=false --dry_run [SQL_QUERY]

Question #225

You are using Cloud Console and want to check on some jobs running in BigQuery. You navigate to the BigQuery part of the console. Which menu item would you click to view jobs?

1. Job History.
2. Active Jobs.
3. My Jobs.
4. You can't view job status in the console; you have to use bq on the command line.

Correct Answer(s):

Job History.

Question #226

You want to estimate the cost of running a BigQuery query. What two services within Google Cloud Platform will you need to use?

1. BigQuery and Billing
2. Billing and Pricing Calculator
3. BigQuery and Pricing Calculator
4. Billing and Pricing Calculator

Correct Answer(s):

BigQuery and Pricing Calculator

Question #227

You have just created a Cloud Spanner instance. You have been tasked with creating a way to store data about a product catalog. What is the next step after creating a Cloud Spanner instance that you would perform to enable you to load data?

1. Run gcloud spanner update-security-patches.
2. Create a database within the instance.
3. Create tables to hold the data.
4. Use the Cloud Spanner console to import data into tables created with the instance.

Correct Answer(s):

Create a database within the instance.

Question #228

You have created a Cloud Spanner instance and database. According to Google best practices,

how often should you update VM packages using apt-get?

1. Every 24 hours.

2. Every 7 days.
3. Every 30 days.
4. Never, Cloud Spanner is a managed service.

Correct Answer(s):

Never, Cloud Spanner is a managed service.

Question #229

Your software team is developing a distributed application and wants to send messages from one application to another. Once the consuming application reads a message, it should be deleteYou want your system to be robust to failure, so messages should be available for at least three days before they are discardeWhich GCP service is best designed to support this use case?

1. Bigtable
2. Dataproc
3. Cloud Pub/Sub
4. Cloud Spanner

Correct Answer(s):

Cloud Pub/Sub

Question #230

Your manager asks you to set up a bare-bones Pub/Sub system as a sandbox for new devel- opers to learn about messaging systems. What are the two resources within Pub/Sub you will need to create?

1. Topics and tables
2. Topics and databases
3. Topics and subscriptions
4. Tables and subscriptions

Correct Answer(s):

Topics and subscriptions

Question #231

Your company is launching an IoT service and will receive large volumes of streaming datYou have to store this data in Bigtable. You want to explore the Bigtable environment from the command line. What command would you run to ensure you have command-line tools installed?

1. apt-get install bigtable-tools
2. apt-get install cbt
3. gcloud components install cbt
4. gcloud components install bigtable-tools

Correct Answer(s):

gcloud components install cbt

Question #232

You need to create a table called iot-ingest-data in Bigtable. What command would you use?

1. cbt createtable iot-ingest-data
2. gcloud bigtable tables create ace-exam-bt-table
3. gcloud bigtable create tables ace-exam-bt-table
4. gcloud create ace-exam-bt-table

Correct Answer(s):

cbt createtable iot-ingest-data

Question #234

Cloud Dataproc is a managed service for which two big data platforms?

1. Spark and Cassandra
2. Spark and Hadoop
3. Hadoop and Cassandra
4. Spark and TensorFlow

Correct Answer(s):

Spark and Hadoop

Question #235

Your department has been asked to analyze large batches of data every night. The jobs will run for about three to four hours. You want to shut down resources as soon as the analysis is done, so you decide to write a script to create a Dataproc cluster every night at midnight. What command would you use to create a cluster called spark-nightly-analysis in the us-west2-a zone?

1. bq dataproc clusters create spark-nightly-analysis --zone us-west2-a
2. gcloud dataproc clusters create spark-nightly-analysis --zone us-west2-a
3. gcloud dataproc clusters spark-nightly-analysis --zone us-west2-a
4. None of the above

Correct Answer(s):

gcloud dataproc clusters create spark-nightly-analysis --zone us-west2-a

Question #236

You have a number of buckets containing old data that is hardly ever useYou don't want to delete it, but you want to minimize the cost of storing it. You decide to change the storage class to coldline for each of those buckets. What is the command structure that you would use?

1. gcloud rewrite -s [STORAGE_CLASS] gs://[PATH_TO_OBJECT]

2. gsutil rewrite -s [STORAGE_CLASS] gs://[PATH_TO_OBJECT]
3. cbt rewrite -s [STORAGE_CLASS] gs://[PATH_TO_OBJECT]
4. bq rewrite -s [STORAGE_CLASS] gs://[PATH_TO_OBJECT]

Correct Answer(s):

gsutil rewrite -s [STORAGE_CLASS] gs://[PATH_TO_OBJECT]

Question #237

You want to rename an object stored in a bucket. What command structure would you use?

1. gsutil   cp   gs://[BUCKET_NAME]/[OLD_OBJECT_NAME] gs://[BUCKET_NAME]/
2. [NEW_OBJECT_NAME]
3. gsutil   mv   gs://[BUCKET_NAME]/[OLD_OBJECT_NAME] gs://[BUCKET_NAME]/ [NEW_OBJECT_NAME]
4. gsutil mv gs://[OLD_OBJECT_NAME] gs://[NEW_OBJECT_NAME]
5. gcloud   mv   gs://[OLD_OBJECT_NAME] gs://[NEW_OBJECT_NAME]

Correct Answer(s):

gsutil   mv   gs://[BUCKET_NAME]/[OLD_OBJECT_NAME] gs://[BUCKET_NAME]/ [NEW_OBJECT_NAME]

Question #238

An executive in your company emails you asking about creating a recommendation system that will help sell more products. The executive has heard there are some GCP solutions that may be good fits for this problem. What GCP service would you recommend the executive look into?

1. Cloud Dataproc, especially Spark and its machine learning library
2. Cloud Dataproc, especially Hadoop
3. Cloud Spanner, which is a global relational database that can hold a lot of data

4. Cloud SQL, because SQL is a powerful query language

Correct Answer(s):

Cloud Dataproc, especially Spark and its machine learning library

Question #239

Which of the following commands is used to create buckets in Cloud Storage?

1. gcloud storage buckets create
2. gsutil storage buckets create
3. gsutil mb
4. gcloud mb

Correct Answer(s):

gsutil mb

Question #240

You need to copy files from your local device to a bucket in Cloud Storage. What command

would you use? Assume you have Cloud SDK installed on your local computer.

1. gsutil copy
2. gsutil cp
3. gcloud cp
4. gcloud storage objects copy

Correct Answer(s):

gsutil cp

Question #241

You are migrating a large number of files from a local storage system to Cloud Storage. You want to use the Cloud Console instead of writing a script. Which of the following Cloud Storage operations can you perform in the console?

1. Upload files only
2. Upload folders only
3. Upload files and folders
4. Compare local files with files in the bucket using the diff command

Correct Answer(s):

Upload files and folders

Question #242

A software developer asks for your help exporting data from a Cloud SQL database. The developer tells you which database to export and which bucket to store the export file in, but hasn't mentioned which file format should be used for the export file. What are the options for the export file format?

1. CSV and XML
2. CSV and JSON
3. JSON and SQL
4. CSV and SQL

Correct Answer(s):

CSV and SQL

Question #243

A database administrator has asked for an export of a MySQL database in Cloud SQL. The database administrator will load the data into another relational database and would to do it with the least amount of work. Specifically, the loading method should not require the database administrator to define a schemWhat file format would you recommend for this task?

1. SQL
2. CSV
3. XML
4. JSON

Correct Answer(s):

SQL

Question #244

Which command will export a MySQL database called ace-exam-mysql1 to a file called

ace-exam-mysql-export.sql in a bucket named ace-exam-buckete1?

1. gcloud storage export sql ace-exam-mysql1 gs://ace-exam-buckete1/ace-
2. exam-mysql-export.sql \ --database=mysql
3. gcloud sql export ace-exam-mysql1 gs://ace-exam-buckete1/ace-exam-mysql-export.sql \ --database=mysql
4. gcloud sql export sql ace-exam-mysql1 gs://ace-exam-buckete1/ace-exam- mysql-export.sql \ --database=mysql
5. gcloud sql export sql ace-exam-mysql1 gs://ace-exam-mysql-export.sql/ ace-exam-buckete1/ \ --database=mysql

Correct Answer(s):

gcloud sql export sql ace-exam-mysql1 gs://ace-exam-buckete1/ace-exam- mysql-export.sql \ --database=mysql

Question #245

As part of a compliance regimen, your team is required to back up data from your Datastore database to an object storage system. Your data is stored in the default namespace. What command would you use to export the default namespace from Datastore to a bucket called ace-exam-bucket1?

1. gcloud datastore export --namespaces="(default)" gs://ace-exam-bucket1

2. gcloud datastore export --namespaces="(default)" ace-exam-bucket1
3. gcloud datastore dump --namespaces="(default)" gs://ace-exam-bucket1
4. gcloud datastore dump --namespaces="(default)" ace-exam-bucket1

Correct Answer(s):

gcloud datastore export --namespaces="(default)" gs://ace-exam-bucket1

Question #246

As required by your company's policy, you need to back up your Datastore database at least once per day. An auditor is questioning whether or not Datastore export is sufficient. You explain that the Datastore export command produces what outputs?

1. A single entity file
2. A metadata file
3. A metadata file and a folder with the data
4. A metadata file, an entity file, and a folder with the data

Correct Answer(s):

A metadata file and a folder with the data

Question #247

Which of the following file formats is not an option for an export file when exporting from BigQuery?

1. CSV
2. XML
3. Avro
4. JSON

Correct Answer(s):

XML

Question #248

Which of the following file formats is not supported when importing data into BigQuery?

1. CSV
2. Parquet
3. Avro
4. YAML

Correct Answer(s):

YAML

Question #249

You have received a large data set from an Internet of Things (IoT) system. You want to use BigQuery to analyze the datWhat command-line command would you use to make data available for analysis in BigQuery?

1. bq   load   --autodetect   --source_format=[FORMAT] [DATASET].[TABLE] [PATH_TO_SOURCE]
2. bq   import   --autodetect   --source_format=[FORMAT] [DATASET].[TABLE] [PATH_TO_SOURCE]
3. gcloud BigQuery load --autodetect --source_format=[FORMAT] [DATASET]. [TABLE] [PATH_TO_SOURCE]
4. gcloud BigQuery load --autodetect --source_format=[FORMAT] [DATASET]. [TABLE] [PATH_TO_SOURCE]

Correct Answer(s):

bq   load   --autodetect   --source_format=[FORMAT]   [DATASET].[TABLE] [PATH_TO_SOURCE]

Question #250

You have set up a Cloud Spanner process to export data to Cloud Storage. You notice that each time the process runs you incur charges for another GCP service, which you think is related to the export process. What other GCP service might be incurring charges during the Cloud Spanner export?

1. Dataproc
2. Dataflow
3. Datastore
4. bq

Correct Answer(s):

Dataflow

Question #251

As a developer on a project using Bigtable for an IoT application, you will need to export data from Bigtable to make some data available for analysis with another tool. What would you use to export the data, assuming you want to minimize the amount of effort required on your part?

1. A Java program designed for importing and exporting data from Bigtable
2. gcloud bigtable table export
3. bq bigtable table export
4. An import tool provided by the analysis tool

Correct Answer(s):

A Java program designed for importing and exporting data from Bigtable

Question #252

You have just exported from a Dataproc cluster. What have you exported?

1. Data in Spark DataFrames
2. All tables in the Spark database
3. Configuration data about the cluster
4. All tables in the Hadoop database

Correct Answer(s):

Configuration data about the cluster

Question #253

A team of data scientists has requested access to data stored in Bigtable so that they can train machine learning models. They explain that Bigtable does not have the features required to build machine learning models. Which of the following GCP services are they most likely to use to build machine learning models?

1. Datastore
2. Dataflow
3. Dataproc
4. DataAnalyze

Correct Answer(s):

Dataproc

Question #254

The correct command to create a Pub/Sub topic is which of the following?

1. gcloud pubsub topics create
2. gcloud pubsub create topics
3. bq pubsub create topics
4. cbt pubsub topics create

Correct Answer(s):

gcloud pubsub topics create

Question #255

Which of the following commands will create a subscription on the topic ace-exam-topic1?

1. gcloud pubsub create --topic=ace-exam-topic1 ace-exam-sub1
2. gcloud pubsub subscriptions create --topic=ace-exam-topic1
3. gcloud pubsub subscriptions create --topic=ace-exam-topic1 ace-exam-sub1
4. gsutil pubsub subscriptions create --topic=ace-exam-topic1 ace-exam-sub1

Correct Answer(s):

gcloud pubsub subscriptions create --topic=ace-exam-topic1 ace-exam-sub1

Question #256

What is one of the direct advantages of using a message queue in distributed systems?

1. It increases security.
2. It decouples services, so if one lags, it does not cause other services to lag.
3. It supports more programming languages.
4. It stores messages until they are read by default.

Correct Answer(s):

It decouples services, so if one lags, it does not cause other services to lag.

Question #257

To ensure you have installed beta gcloud commands, which command should you run?

1. gcloud components beta install
2. gcloud components install beta
3. gcloud commands install beta

4. gcloud commands beta install

Correct Answer(s):

gcloud components install beta

Question #258

What parameter is used to tell BigQuery to automatically detect the schema of a file on

import?

1. --autodetect
2. --autoschema
3. --detectschema
4. --dry_run

Correct Answer(s):

--autodetect

Question #259

The compression options deflate and snappy are available for what file types when exporting from BigQuery?

1. Avro
2. CSV
3. XML
4. Thrift

Correct Answer(s):

Avro

Question #260

Virtual private clouds have a _____ scope.

1. Zonal
2. Regional
3. Super-regional
4. Global

Correct Answer(s):

Global

Question #261

You have been tasked with defining CIDR ranges to use with a project. The project includes 2 VPCs with several subnets in each VPHow many CIDR ranges will you need to define?

1. One for each VPC
2. One for each subnet
3. One for each region
4. One for each zone

Correct Answer(s):

One for each subnet

Question #262

The legal department needs to isolate its resources on its own VPYou want to have network provide routing to any other service available on the global network. The VPC network has not learned global routes. What parameter may have been missed when creating the VPC subnets?

1. DNS server policy
2. Dynamic routing
3. Static routing policy

4. Systemic routing policy

Correct Answer(s):

Dynamic routing

Question #263

The command to create a VPC from the command line is:

1. gcloud compute networks create
2. gcloud networks vpc create
3. gsutil networks vpc create
4. gcloud compute create networks

Correct Answer(s):

gcloud compute networks create

Question #264

You have created several subnets. Most of them are sending logs to Stackdriver. One subnet is not sending logs. What option may have been misconfigured when creating the subnet that is not forwarding logs?

1. Flow Logs
2. Private IP Access
3. Stackdriver Logging
4. Variable-Length Subnet Masking

Correct Answer(s):

Flow Logs

Question #265

At what levels of the resource hierarchy can a shared VPC be created?

1. Folders and resources
2. Organizations and project
3. Organizations and folders
4. Folders and subnets

Correct Answer(s):

Organizations and folders

Question #266

You are using Cloud Console to create a VM that you want to exist in a custom subnet you just createWhat section of the Create Instance form would you use to specify the custom subnet?

1. Networking tab of the Management, Security, Disks, Networking, Sole Tenancy section
2. Management tab of the Management, Security, Disks, Networking, Sole Tenancy section
3. Sole Tenancy tab of Management, Security, Disks, Networking, Sole Tenancy
4. Sole Tenancy tab of Management, Security, Disks, Networking

Correct Answer(s):

Networking tab of the Management, Security, Disks, Networking, Sole Tenancy section

Question #267

You want to implement interproject communication between VPCs. Which feature of VPCs would you use to implement this?

1. VPC peering

2. Interproject peering
3. VPN
4. Interconnect

Correct Answer(s):

VPC peering

Question #268

You want to limit traffic to a set of instances. You decide to set a specific network tag on each instance. What part of a firewall rule can reference the network tag to determine the set of instances affected by the rule?

1. Action
2. Target
3. Priority
4. Direction

Correct Answer(s):

Target

Question #269

What part of a firewall rule determines whether a rule applies to incoming or outgoing traffic?

1. Action
2. Target
3. Priority
4. Direction

Correct Answer(s):

Direction

Question #270

You want to define a CIDR range that applies to all destination addresses. What IP address would you specify?

1. 0.0.0.0/0
2. 10.0.0.0/8
3. 172.16.0.0/12
4. 192.168.0.0/16

Correct Answer(s):

0.0.0.0/0

Question #271

You are using gcloud to create a firewall rule. Which command would you use?

1. gcloud network firewall-rules create
2. gcloud compute firewall-rules create
3. gcloud network rules create
4. gcloud compute rules create

Correct Answer(s):

gcloud compute firewall-rules create

Question #272

You are using gcloud to create a firewall rule. Which parameter would you use to specify

the subnet it should apply to?

1. --subnet
2. --network
3. --destination
4. --source-ranges

--network

Question #273

An application development team is deploying a set of specialized service endpoints and wants to limit traffic so that only traffic going to one of the endpoints is allowed through by firewall rules. The service endpoints will accept any UDP traffic and each endpoint will use a port in the range of 20000-30000. Which of the following commands would you use?

1. gcloud compute firewall-rules create fwr1 --allow=udp:20000-30000 -- direction=ingress
2. gcloud network firewall-rules create fwr1 --allow=udp:20000-30000 -- direction=ingress
3. gcloud compute firewall-rules create fwr1 --allow=udp
4. gcloud compute firewall-rules create fwr1 --direction=ingress

Correct Answer(s):

gcloud compute firewall-rules create fwr1 --allow=udp:20000-30000 -- direction=ingress

Question #274

You have a rule to allow inbound traffic to a VM. You want it to apply only if there is not another rule that would deny that traffiWhat priority should you give this rule?

1. 0
2. 1
3. 1000
4. 65535

Correct Answer(s):

65535

Question #275

You want to create a VPN using Cloud Console. What section of Cloud Console should you use?

1. Compute Engine
2. App Engine
3. Hybrid Connectivity
4. IAM & Admin

Correct Answer(s):

Hybrid Connectivity

Question #276

You are using Cloud Console to create a VPN. You want to configure the GCP end of the VPN. What section of the Create VPN form would you use?

1. Tunnels
2. Routing Options
3. Google Compute Engine VPN
4. IKE Version

Correct Answer(s):

Google Compute Engine VPN

Question #277

You want the router on a tunnel you are creating to learn routes from all GCP regions on the network. What feature of GCP routing would you enable?

1. Global dynamic routing
2. Regional routing
3. VPC
4. Firewall rules

Correct Answer(s):

Global dynamic routing

Question #278

When you create a cloud router, what kind of unique identifier do you need to assign for the BGP protocol?

1. IP address
2. ASN
3. Dynamic load routing ID
4. None of the above

Correct Answer(s):

ASN

Question #279

You are using gcloud to create a VPN. Which command would you use?

1. gcloud compute target-vpn-gateways only
2. gcloud compute forwarding-rule and gcloud compute target-vpn-gateways only
3. gcloud compute vpn-tunnels only
4. gcloud compute forwarding-rule, gcloud compute target-vpn-gateways, and gcloud compute vpn-tunnels

Correct Answer(s):

gcloud compute forwarding-rule, gcloud compute target-vpn-gateways, and gcloud compute vpn-tunnels

Question #280

What record type is used to specify the IPv4 address of a domain?

1. AAAA
2. A
3. NS
4. SOA

Correct Answer(s):

A

Question #281

The CEO of your startup just read a news report about a company that was attacked by something called cache poisoning. The CEO wants to implement additional security measures to reduce the risk of DNS spoofing and cache poisoning. What would you recommend?

1. Using DNSSEC
2. Adding SOA records
3. Adding CNAME records
4. Deleting CNAME records

Correct Answer(s):

Using DNSSEC

Question #282

What do the TTL parameters specify in a DNS record?

1. Time a record can exist in a cache before it should be queried again
2. Time a client has to respond to a request for DNS information
3. Time allowed to create a CNAME record
4. Time before a human has to manually verify the information in the DNS record

Correct Answer(s):

Time a record can exist in a cache before it should be queried again

Question #283

What command is used to create a DNS zone in the command line?

1. gsutil dns managed-zones create
2. gcloud dns managed-zones create
3. gcloud beta managed-zones create
4. gcloud beta dns create managed zones

Correct Answer(s):

gcloud dns managed-zones create

Question #284

What parameter is used to make a DNS zone private?

1. --private
2. --visibility=private
3. --private=true
4. --status=private

Correct Answer(s):

--visibility=private

Question #285

Which load balancers provide global load balancing?

1. HTTP(S) only
2. SSL Proxy and TCP Proxy only
3. HTTP(S), SSL Proxy, and TCP Proxy
4. Internal TCP/UDP, HTTP(S), SSL Proxy, and TCP Proxy

Correct Answer(s):

HTTP(S), SSL Proxy, and TCP Proxy

Question #286

Which regional load balancer allows for load balancing based on IP protocol, address, and port?

1. HTTP(S)
2. SSL Proxy
3. TCP Proxy
4. Network TCP/UDP

Correct Answer(s):

Network TCP/UDP

Question #287

You are configuring a load balancer and want to implement private load balancing. Which option would you select?

1. Only Between My VMs

2. Enable Private
3. Disable Public
4. Local Only

Correct Answer(s):

Only Between My VMs

Question #288

What two components need to be configured when creating a TCP Proxy load balancer?

1. Frontend and forwarding rule
2. Frontend and backend
3. Forwarding rule and backend only
4. Backend and forwarding rule only

Correct Answer(s):

Frontend and backend

Question #289

A health check is used to check what resources?

1. Load balancer
2. VMs
3. Storage buckets
4. Persistent disks

Correct Answer(s):

VMs

Question #290

Where do you specify the ports on a TCP Proxy load balancer that should have their traffic forwarded?

1. Backend
2. Frontend
3. Network Services section
4. VPC

Correct Answer(s):

Frontend

Question #291

What command is used to create a network load balancer at the command line?

1. gcloud compute forwarding-rules create
2. gcloud network forwarding-rules create
3. gcloud compute create forwarding-rules
4. gcloud network create forwarding-rules

Correct Answer(s):

gcloud compute forwarding-rules create

Question #292

A team is setting up a web service for internal use. They want to use the same IP address for

the foreseeable future. What type of IP address would you assign?

1. Internal
2. External
3. Static
4. Ephemeral

Correct Answer(s):

Static

Question #293

You are starting up a VM to experiment with a new Python data science library. You'll SSH via the server name into the VM, use the Python interpreter interactively for a while and then shut down the machine. What type of IP address would you assign to this VM?

1. Ephemeral
2. Static
3. Permanent
4. IPv8

Correct Answer(s):

Ephemeral

Question #294

You have created a subnet called sn1 using 192.168.0.0 with 65,534 addresses. You realize that you will not need that many addresses, and you'd like to reduce that number to 254. Which of the following commands would you use?

1. gcloud compute networks subnets expand-ip-range sn1 --prefix-length=24
2. gcloud compute networks subnets expand-ip-range sn1 --prefix-length=-8
3. gcloud compute networks subnets expand-ip-range sn1 --size=256
4. There is no command to reduce the number of IP addresses available.

Correct Answer(s):

There is no command to reduce the number of IP addresses available.

Question #295

You have created a subnet called sn1 using 192.168.0.0. You want it to have 14 addresses. What prefix length would you use?

1. 32
2. 28
3. 20
4. 16

Correct Answer(s):

28

Question #296

You want all your network traffic to route over the Google network and not traverse the public Internet. What level of network service should you choose?

1. Standard
2. Google-only
3. Premium
4. Non-Internet

Correct Answer(s):

Premium

Question #297

You have a website hosted on a Compute Engine VM. Users can access the website using the domain name you provideYou do some maintenance work on the VM and stop the server and restart it. Now users cannot access the website. No other changes have occurred on the subnet. What might be the cause of the problem?

1. The restart caused a change in the DNS record.
2. You used an ephemeral instead of a static IP address.

3. You do not have enough addresses available on your subnet.
4. Your subnet has changed.

Correct Answer(s):

You used an ephemeral instead of a static IP address.

Question #298

You are deploying a distributed system. Messages will be passed between Compute Engine VMs using a reliable UDP protocol. All VMs are in the same region. You want to use the load balancer that best fits these requirements. Which kind of load balancer would you use?

1. Internal TCP/UDP
2. TCP Proxy
3. SSL Proxy
4. HTTP(S)

Correct Answer(s):

Internal TCP/UDP

Question #299

You want to use Cloud Console to review the records in a DNS entry. What section of Cloud Console would you navigate to?

1. Compute Engine
2. Network Services
3. Kubernetes Engine
4. Hybrid Connectivity

Correct Answer(s):

Network Services

Question #300

What are the categories of Cloud Launcher solutions?

1. Data sets only
2. Operating systems only
3. Developer tools and operating systems only
4. Data sets, operating systems, and developer tools

Correct Answer(s):

Data sets, operating systems, and developer tools

Question #301

What is the other name of Cloud Launcher?

1. Cloud Deployment Manager
2. Marketplace
3. Cloud Tools
4. Cloud Solutions: Third Party

Correct Answer(s):

Marketplace

Question #302

Where do you navigate to launch a Cloud Launcher solution?

1. Overview page of the solution
2. Main Cloud Launcher page
3. Network Services
4. None of the above

Correct Answer(s):

Overview page of the solution

Question #303

You want to quickly identify the set of operating systems available in Cloud Launcher.

Which of these steps would help with that?

1. Use Google Search to search the Web for a listing.
2. Use filters in Cloud Launcher.
3. Scroll through the list of solutions displayed on the start page of Cloud Launcher.
4. It is not possible to filter to operating systems.

Correct Answer(s):

Use filters in Cloud Launcher.

Question #304

You want to use Cloud Launcher to deploy a WordPress site. You notice there is more than one WordPress option. Why is that?

1. It's a mistake. Submit a ticket to Google support.
2. Multiple vendors may offer the same application.
3. It's a mistake. Submit a ticket to the vendors.
4. You will never see such an option.

Correct Answer(s):

Multiple vendors may offer the same application.

Question #305

You have used Cloud Launcher to deploy a WordPress site and would now like to deploy a database. You notice that the configuration form for the databases is different from the form used with WordPress. Why is that?

1. It's a mistake. Submit a ticket to Google support.
2. You've navigated to a different subform of Cloud Launcher.
3. Configuration properties are based on the application you are deploying and will be different depending on what application you are deploying.
4. This cannot happen.

Correct Answer(s):

Configuration properties are based on the application you are deploying and will be different depending on what application you are deploying.

Question #306

You have been asked by your manager to deploy a WordPress site. You expect heavy traffic, and your manager wants to make sure the VM hosting the WordPress site has enough resources. Which resources can you configure when launching a WordPress site using Cloud Launcher?

1. Machine type
2. Disk type
3. Disk size
4. All of the above

Correct Answer(s):

All of the above

Question #307

You would like to define as code the configuration of a set of application resources. The GCP service for creating resources using a configuration file made up of resource specifications defined in YAML syntax is called what?

1. Compute Engine
2. Deployment Manager
3. Marketplace Manager
4. Marketplace Deployer

Correct Answer(s):

Deployment Manager

Question #308

What file format is used to define Deployment Manager configuration files?

1. XML
2. JSON
3. CSV
4. YAML

Correct Answer(s):

YAML

Question #309

A Deployment Manager configuration file starts with what term?

1. Deploy
2. Resources
3. Properties
4. YAML

Correct Answer(s):

Resources

Question #310

Which of the following are used to define a resource in a Cloud Deployment Manager configuration file?

1. type only
2. properties only
3. name and type only
4. type, properties, and name

Correct Answer(s):

type, properties, and name

Question #311

What properties may be set when defining a disk on a VM?

1. A device name only
2. A Boolean indicating a boot disk and a Boolean indicating autodelete
3. A Boolean indicating autodelete only
4. A device name, a Boolean indicating a boot disk, and a Boolean indicating autodelete

Correct Answer(s):

A device name, a Boolean indicating a boot disk, and a Boolean indicating autodelete

Question #312

You need to look up what images are available in the zone in which you want to deploy a VM. What command would you use?

1. gcloud compute images list
2. gcloud images list
3. gsutil compute images list
4. gcloud compute list images

Correct Answer(s):

gcloud compute images list

Question #313

You want to use a template file with Deployment Manager. You expect the file to be complicateWhat language would you use?

1. Jinja2
2. Ruby
3. Go
4. Python

Correct Answer(s):

Python

Question #314

What command launches a deployment?

1. gcloud deployment-manager deployments create
2. gcloud cloud-launcher deployments create
3. gcloud deployment-manager deployments launch
4. gcloud cloud-launcher deployments launch

Correct Answer(s):

gcloud deployment-manager deployments create

Question #315

A DevOps engineer is noticing a spike in CPU utilization on your servers. You explain you have just launched a deployment. You'd like to show the DevOps engineer the details of a deployment you just launcheWhat command would you use?

1. gcloud cloud-launcher deployments describe
2. gcloud deployment-manager deployments list
3. gcloud deployment-manager deployments describe
4. gcloud cloud-launcher deployments list

Correct Answer(s):

gcloud deployment-manager deployments describe

Question #316

If you expand the More link in the Networking section when deploying a Cloud Launcher solution, what will you be able to configure?

1. IP addresses
2. Billing
3. Access controls
4. Custom machine type

Correct Answer(s):

IP addresses

Question #317

What are the license types referenced in Cloud Launcher?

1. Free only
2. Free and Paid only
3. Free and Bring your own license (BYOL) only
4. Free, paid, and bring your own license

Correct Answer(s):

Free, paid, and bring your own license

Question #318

Which license type will add charges to your GCP bill when using Cloud Launcher with this

1. type of license?
2. Free
3. Paid
4. BYOL
5. Chargeback

Correct Answer(s):

Paid

Question #319

You are deploying a Cloud Launcher application that includes a LAMP stack. What software will this deploy?

1. Apache server and Linux only
2. Linux only
3. MySQL and Apache only
4. Apache, MySQL, Linux, and PHP

Correct Answer(s):

Apache, MySQL, Linux, and PHP

Question #320

What does IAM stand for?

1. Identity and Authorization Management
2. Identity and Access Management
3. Identity and Auditing Management
4. Individual Access Management

Correct Answer(s):

Identity and Access Management

Question #321

When you navigate to IAM & Admin in Cloud Console, what appears in the main body of the page?

1. Members and roles assigned
2. Roles only
3. Members only
4. Roles and permissions assigned

Correct Answer(s):

Members and roles assigned

Question #322

Why are primitive roles classified in a category in addition to IAM?

1. They are part of IAM.
2. They were created before IAM.
3. They were created after IAM.
4. They are not related to access control.

Correct Answer(s):

They were created before IAM.

Question #323

A developer intern is confused about what roles are used for. You describe IAM roles as a collection of what?

1. Identities
2. Permissions
3. Access control lists
4. Audit logs

Correct Answer(s):

Permissions

Question #324

You want to list roles assigned to users in a project called ace-exam-project. What gcloud command would you use?

1. gcloud iam get-iam-policy ace-exam-project
2. gcloud projects list ace-exam-project
3. gcloud projects get-iam-policy ace-exam-project
4. gcloud iam list ace-exam-project

Correct Answer(s):

gcloud projects get-iam-policy ace-exam-project

Question #325

You are working in the form displayed after clicking the Add link in the IAM form of IAM & Admin in Cloud Console. There is a parameter called New Members. What items would you enter in that parameter?

1. Individual users only
2. Individual users or groups
3. Roles or individual users
4. Roles or groups

Correct Answer(s):

Individual users or groups

Question #326

You have been assigned the App Engine Deployer role. What operations can you perform?

1. Write new versions of an application only
2. Read application configuration and settings only
3. Read application configuration and settings and write new configurations
4. Read application configuration and settings and write new versions

Correct Answer(s):

Read application configuration and settings and write new versions

Question #327

You want to list permissions in a role using Cloud Console. Where would you go to see that?

1. IAM & Admin; select Roles. All permissions will be displayed.
2. IAM & Admin; select Roles. Check the box next to a role to display the permissions in that role.
3. IAM & Admin; select Audit Logs.
4. IAM & Admin; select Service Accounts and then Roles.

Correct Answer(s):

IAM & Admin; select Roles. Check the box next to a role to display the permissions in that role.

Question #328

You are meeting with an auditor to discuss security practices in the clouThe auditor asks how you implement several best practices. You describe how IAM predefined roles help to implement which security best practice(s)?

1. Least privilege
2. Separation of duties
3. Defense in depth
4. Options A and B

Correct Answer(s):

Options A and B

Question #329

What launch stages are available when creating custom roles?

1. Alpha and beta only
2. General availability only
3. Disabled only
4. Alpha, beta, general availability, and disabled

Correct Answer(s):

Alpha, beta, general availability, and disabled

Question #330

The gcloud command to create a custom role is what?

1. gcloud project roles create
2. gcloud iam roles create
3. gcloud project create roles
4. gcloud iam create roles

Correct Answer(s):

gcloud iam roles create

Question #331

A DevOps engineer is confused about the purpose of scopes. Scopes are access controls that are applied to what kind of resources?

1. Storage buckets
2. VM instances
3. Persistent disks
4. Subnets

Correct Answer(s):

VM instances

Question #332

A scope is identified using what kind of identifier?

1. A randomly generated ID
2. A URL beginning with https://www.googleserviceaccounts/
3. A URL beginning with https://www.googleapis.com/auth/
4. A URL beginning with https://www.googleapis.com/auth/PROJECT_ID]

Correct Answer(s):

A URL beginning with https://www.googleapis.com/auth/

Question #333

A VM instance is trying to read from a Cloud Storage bucket. Reading the bucket is allowed by IAM roles granted to the service account of the VM. Reading buckets is denied by the scopes assigned to the VM. What will happen if the VM tries to read from the bucket?

1. The application performing the read will skip over the read operation.
2. The read will execute because the most permissive permission is allowed.
3. The read will not execute because both scopes and IAM roles are applied to determine what operations can be performed.
4. The read operation will succeed, but a message will be logged to Stackdriver Logging.

Correct Answer(s):

The read will not execute because both scopes and IAM roles are applied to determine what operations can be performed.

Question #334

What are the options for setting scopes in a VM?

1. Allow Default Access and Allow Full Access only
2. Allow Default Access, Allow Full Access, and Set Access for Each API
3. Allow Full Access or Set Access For Each API only
4. Allow Default Access and Set Access For Each API only

Correct Answer(s):

Allow Default Access, Allow Full Access, and Set Access for Each API

Question #335

What gcloud command would you use to set scopes?

1. gcloud compute instances set-scopes
2. gcloud compute instances set-service-account
3. gcloud compute service-accounts set-scopes
4. gcloud compute service-accounts define-scopes

Correct Answer(s):

gcloud compute instances set-service-account

Question #336

What gcloud command would you use to assign a service account when creating a VM?

1. gcloud compute instances create [INSTANCE_NAME]
2. --service-account [SERVICE_ACCOUNT_EMAIL]
3. gcloud compute instances create-service-account [INSTANCE_NAME][SERVICE_ACCOUNT_EMAIL]
4. gcloud compute instances define-service-account [INSTANCE_NAME][SERVICE_ACCOUNT_EMAIL]
5. gcloud compute create instances-service-account [INSTANCE_NAME][SERVICE_ACCOUNT_EMAIL]

Correct Answer(s):

gcloud compute instances create [INSTANCE_NAME] --service-account

Question #337

What GCP service is used to view audit logs?

1. Compute Engine
2. Cloud Storage
3. Stackdriver Logging
4. Custom logging

Correct Answer(s):

Stackdriver Logging

Question #338

What options are available for filtering log messages when viewing audit logs?

1. Period time and log level only
2. Resource, type of log, log level, and period of time only
3. Resource and period of time only
4. Type of log only

Correct Answer(s):

Resource, type of log, log level, and period of time only

Question #339

An auditor needs to review audit logs. You assign read-only permission to a custom role you create for auditors. What security best practice are you following?

1. Defense in depth
2. Least privilege
3. Separation of duties
4. Vulnerability scanning

Correct Answer(s):

Least privilege

Question #340

What Stackdriver service is used to generate alerts when the CPU utilization of a VM exceeds 80 percent?

1. Logging
2. Monitoring
3. Cloud Trace
4. Cloud Debug

Correct Answer(s):

Monitoring

Question #341

You have just created a virtual machine, and you'd like Stackdriver Monitoring to alert you via email whenever the CPU average utilization exceeds 75 percent for 5 minutes. What do you need to do to the VM to have this happen?

1. Install a Stackdriver workspace
2. Install the Stackdriver monitoring agent on the VM
3. Edit the VM configuration in Cloud Console and check the Monitor With Stackdriver checkbox
4. Set a notification channel

Correct Answer(s):

Install the Stackdriver monitoring agent on the VM

Question #342

Stackdriver can be used to monitor resources where?

1. In Google Cloud Platform only
2. In Google Cloud Platform and Amazon Web Services only
3. In Google Cloud Platform and on premises data centers
4. In Google Cloud Platform, Amazon Web Services, and on premises data centers

Correct Answer(s):

In Google Cloud Platform, Amazon Web Services, and on premises data centers

Question #343

Grouping a set of metrics that arrive in a period of time into regular-sized buckets is called what?

1. Aggregation
2. Alignment
3. Minimization
4. Consolidation

Correct Answer(s):

Alignment

Question #344

You have created a condition of CPU utilization, and you want to receive notifications. Which of the following are options?

1. Email only
2. PagerDuty only
3. Hipchat and PagerDuty
4. Email, PagerDuty, and Hipchat

Correct Answer(s):

Email, PagerDuty, and Hipchat

Question #345

When you create a policy to notify you of a potential problem with your infrastructure, you can specify optional documentation. Why would you bother putting documentation in that form?

1. It is saved to Cloud Storage for future use.
2. It can help you or a colleague understand the purpose of the policy.
3. It can contain information that would help someone diagnose and correct the problem.

4. Options B and C.

Correct Answer(s):

Options B and C.

Question #346

What is alert fatigue, and why is it a problem?

1. Too many alert notifications are sent for events that do not require human intervention, and eventually DevOps engineers begin to pay less attention to notifications.
2. Too many alerts put unnecessary load on your systems.
3. Too few alerts leave DevOps engineers uncertain of the state of your applications and
4. infrastructure.
5. Too many false alerts

Correct Answer(s):

Too many alert notifications are sent for events that do not require human intervention, and eventually DevOps engineers begin to pay less attention to notifications.

Question #347

How long is log data stored in Stackdriver Logging?

1. 7 days
2. 15 days
3. 30 days
4. 60 days

Correct Answer(s):

30 days

Question #348

You need to store log entries for a longer period of time than Stackdriver Logging retains them. What is the best option for preserving log data?

1. There is no option; once the data retention period passes, Stackdriver Logging deletes the data.
2. Create a log sink and export the log data using Stackdriver Logging's export functionality.
3. Write a Python script to use the Stackdriver API to write the data to Cloud Storage.
4. Write a Python script to use the Stackdriver API to write the data to BigQuery.

Correct Answer(s):

Create a log sink and export the log data using Stackdriver Logging's export functionality.

Question #349

Which of the following are options for logging sinks?

1. Cloud Storage bucket only
2. BigQuery dataset and Cloud Storage bucket only
3. Cloud Pub/Sub topic only
4. Cloud Storage bucket, BigQuery dataset, and Cloud Pub/Sub topic

Correct Answer(s):

Cloud Storage bucket, BigQuery dataset, and Cloud Pub/Sub topic

Question #350

Which of the following can be used to filter log entries when viewing logs in Stackdriver Logging?

1. Label or text search only

2. Resource type and log type only
3. Time and resource type only
4. Label or text search, resource type, log type, and time

Correct Answer(s):

Label or text search, resource type, log type, and time

Question #351

Which of the following is not a standard log level that can be used to filter log viewings?

1. Critical
2. Halted
3. Warning
4. Info

Correct Answer(s):

Halted

Question #352

You are viewing log entries and spot one that looks suspicious. You are not familiar with the kind of log entry, and you want to see the complete details of the log entry as quickly as possible. What would you do?

1. Drill down one by one into each structure in the log entry.
2. Click Expand all to show all details.
3. Write a Python script to reformat the log entry.
4. Click the Show Detail link next to the log entry.

Correct Answer(s):

Click Expand all to show all details.

Question #353

What Stackdriver service is best for identifying where bottlenecks exist in your application?

1. Monitoring
2. Logging
3. Trace
4. Debug

Correct Answer(s):

Trace

Question #354

There is a bug in a microservice. You have reviewed application outputs but cannot identify the problem. You decide you need to step through the code. What Stackdriver service would you use to give you insight into the status of the services at particular points in execution?

1. Monitoring
2. Logging
3. Trace
4. Debug

Correct Answer(s):

Debug

Question #355

You believe there may be a problem with BigQuery in the us-central zone. Where would you go to check the status of the BigQuery service for the quickest access to details?

1. Email Google Cloud Support.
2. Check https://status.cloud.google.com/.

3. Check https://bigquery.status.cloud.google.com/.
4. Call Google tech support.

Correct Answer(s):

Check https://status.cloud.google.com/.

Question #356

You would like to estimate the cost of GCP resources you will be using. Which services would

require you to have information on the virtual machines you will be using?

1. Compute Engine and BigQuery
2. Compute Engine and Kubernetes Engine
3. BigQuery and Kubernetes Engine
4. BigQuery and Cloud Pub/Sub

Correct Answer(s):

Compute Engine and Kubernetes Engine

Question #357

You are generating an estimate of the cost of using BigQuery. One of the parameters is Query Pricing. You have to specify a value in TB units. What is the value you are specifying?

1. The amount of data stored in BigQuery
2. The amount of data returned by the query
3. The amount of data scanned by the query
4. The amount of data in Cloud Storage bucket

Correct Answer(s):

The amount of data scanned by the query

Question #358

Why do you need to specify the operating system to be used when estimating the cost of a VM?

1. All operating systems are charged a fixed rate.
2. Some operating systems incur a cost.
3. It's not necessary; it is only included for documentation.
4. To estimate the cost of Bring Your Own License configurations.

Correct Answer(s):

Some operating systems incur a cost.

Question #359

You want to create a custom metric for use in Stackdriver Monitoring but do not want to use the low-level Stackdriver API. What is an alternative open source option for working with custom metrics?

1. Prometheus
2. OpenCensus
3. Grafana
4. Nagios

Correct Answer(s):

OpenCensus

www.ingramcontent.com/pod-product-compliance
Lightning Source LLC
Chambersburg PA
CBHW071251050326
40690CB00011B/2348